PLEASE COME HOME DAD

Eggert Thomsen

Please Come Home Dad
Copyright © 2020 by Eggert Thomsen

Library of Congress Control Number:	2020912730
ISBN-13: Paperback:	978-1-64749-186-4
epub:	978-1-64749-187-1

All rights reserved. No part of this publication may be reproduced, distributed, or transmitted in any form or by any means, including photocopying, recording, or other electronic or mechanical methods, without the prior written permission of the publisher or author, except in the case of brief quotations embodied in critical reviews and certain other noncommercial uses permitted by copyright law.

Although every precaution has been taken to verify the accuracy of the information contained herein, the author and publisher assume no responsibility for any errors or omissions.No liability is assumed for damages that may result from the use of information contained within.

Printed in the United States of America

GoToPublish LLC
1-888-337-1724
www.gotopublish.com
info@gotopublish.com

Well, it's closing time and time to go home after a day's work. I just don't know if I should go home, In fact, I just can't put up with her abuse much longer. 1 know that once I wall in the door she will jump all over me. I don't know what to do about it. I usually just quickly eat supper and head for the basement or out in the garage.

I sometimes ask her, "What is it?" You want me out of here or do you have someone else? She usually replies, "Oh, there you go again". I can never find out what the problem is. It seems that I can't eat right, walk right, or drive right or even talk right. There is something wrong with almost everything I do. Most nights, I just lay there, trying to figure out how to correct whatever it is that I do wrong. She is so good and kind to everyone except me. This hurts because we have had all those good years together. I don't really tell anybody about what is going on, except my oldest son. He is a partner in our business and knows how much I hate to go home after work. Many times, I have had tears and have felt so downhearted.

I knew if had to do something because my thoughts were sometimes drastic. I cannot divorce her. My family means so much to me and I know what I plan to do will hurt my family but it would be the least drastic.

I decided to leave. My plans were to leave with the clothes on my back and about $10 in my pocket. I will leave her a note telling her that I had left her. In the note, I told her that she could use my Social Security money and my pension check and of course, her Social Security checks to live on. These are all direct deposited to our bank account. I would not touch any of it and she would be free of me.

I got up early the next morning at about 4 o'clock. Quietly, I dressed making as little noise as possible, I went out the door. I did not take the car, and I walked the four blocks down to the highway towards a nearby city. I walled about 2 miles. A truck driver stopped to ask if I needed help or did I need a ride. I was very happy to take his offer. I climbed into the cab of the truck and thanked him for being so considerate and helpful. On the way we talked about his family and I could tell that they were very important to him and I asked him if he would drop me off at the truck stop. I did not unload any of my problems on him I just told him that I wanted to be on my own and have some peace. I asked if he could drop me off at the truck stop. He dropped me off at the truck stop and I thanked him again for his help but I was my intention to see if I could hitch a ride with an over the road trucker that may be heading south to Texas or Arizona or that general direction.

He stopped to get lunch and he asked if I wanted some lunch, but I told him I wasn't really hungry, but he said, "I know you have to be hungry, come in the cafeteria with me. Lunch will be on me". It was somewhat embarrassing but he was right, I was very hungry and so thankful to him for his consideration. The more we were together it became obvious what a decent and kind person he is.

We got to Oklahoma City and pulled into the manufacturing company with the load that was to be unloaded there. He and I talked and it was like we had become good friends. He said he was to pick up another load to take to Chicago which was in the wrong direction for me.

I thanked him for all his kindness and wished him well. Before he left, he told me to hang around this manufacturing company because there possibly could be a truck going toward Texas. I waited around the manufacturing company and talked to several of the truckers, but none were going in the direction I needed to go. Most of them were not allowed to take riders anyway. So I walked to a truck stop which was about 3 miles away. 'There were a lot of trucks there so I went into the truck stop and walked up to some of the guys that looked like they were truckers and I inquired about the possibility of riding with anybody that may be heading toward Texas,

My reception wasn't too good; in fact some of them were quite rude and tough acting. Not to the point of telling me to leave them alone but that was a feeling I got. I went outside and stood there surveying the situation I saw a trucker heading for his truck. I went up to him and asked where he was going. He said, "I'm heading for Dallas Texas". That was ideal for me and I asked if it was possible to hitch a ride with him. He didn't seem too enthused about the idea but then he said, "Yeah, I'll take you a long". "You don't look like you would be too much trouble". I said to him, "I sure appreciate this". I climbed into the cab and we were headed for Dallas, Texas. The driver was kind of a big guy with a rough disposition. His language was typical of most truck drivers.

The driver asked, "what the hell are you doing hitching rides"? I explained to him that I was getting away from a difficult marriage situation. He said, "You're not running away from the law are you"? I told him, "No, I just couldn't take the Treatment from the mean wife anymore'.

Having not shaved for a few days, and my clothes were beginning to look rumpled and somewhat dirty. I guess I pretty much looked like a bum.

We arrived in Dallas and pulled into a warehouse where the truck was to be unloaded. I thanked the driver. He said, "good luck to you buddy". As I walked away, I could see sort of a grin on his face. I walked about 5 miles to the downtown area. It was getting late in the day and my thoughts were of finding a place to sleep for the night. Not being familiar with Dallas, I did not know where to look to find either shelter or food. As I was walking toward the downtown, I passed a small Park, so I went in there and found a bench that was not too conspicuous from the street. I lay down on the bench and spent the night there.

I woke up the next morning feeling rested and very hungry. I walked several blocks down the street toward the city hoping that I can find a soup kitchen or someone that would direct me there. I was looking for a particular type of person that may have had experience with a soup kitchen. I talked to several people but they were not interested in conversing with someone that looked like a bum. Finally, I ran into an old man that looked like he may have had some experience with the soup kitchen. I asked him if he could direct me to a shelter. He said to me, "I can do better than that'. He walked with me to the soup kitchen. It was early in the morning and they were still serving breakfast. We went into the soup kitchen and I was surprised at how well they treated me and did their best to make sure that I have been well fed. I also asked him if they would have a place to sleep for a short period of time. 'They said, "Yes, it is only about three blocks down the street". 'They also advised me to get there early because sometimes they fill up quickly I have a lot of time before I have to be there at the shelter to be assured of a bed. My idea was to see if I could find some kind of work in a restaurant, washing dishes or any menial job that would be available. I stopped into several of the restaurants, but was told to move on. They had no interest in hiring a transient. I decided to change my strategy. I went down the street and saw a kind of run down bar, pool hall type of business. I went up to the bar and talked to a person that appeared to be the owner. I explained my situation and told him that 1 would do any kind of work that he needed done. He thought for a minute and said, "well, I could use some one around here to sweep up, empty the trash cans, cleaning the spit tunes and do just general cleaning". He said, "I can only pay you about five dollars an hour and you would work about six hours a day". I readily accepted the job and he told me to be there the next morning at 8 o'clock. I also asked the owner, "is it possible to pay me daily since I have no money"? He said, "yes that would be no problem".

That evening, I went to the shelter after visiting the soup kitchen. I stayed there and it was not as deprecating as I thought it might be. After a couple weeks, I began to have a little money. so I inquired about some cheap housing. I talked to several people and they sent me to a company that took care of renting out low-rent properties. They took me into a building and showed me a small one room apartment that had a bathroom. It is located in a basement and it rented for only $20 per week. It was furnished with a stove, refrigerator and a couch. There also was a small kitchen table and two chairs. After looking at it, I told them I would take it. This would give me some kind of a home and a place to relax in. I moved in and with a little elbow grease, it became somewhat livable and even comfortable.

Meanwhile, at home, my wife woke up and went downstairs expecting to see me; however, she found my note. She did not know what to think. She looked out the window and saw that the car was still there. She went into the basement, I wasn't there either. She went to the phone and called my son. He answered, and she asked, "Have you seen your dad"? "I can't find him anywhere and he left a note saying that he was leaving". "Can you please come here and help me"? My son lives across town, so it took a little time for him to get there. When he finally arrived, his mother was quite shook up. My son read the note and said to his mother, "I was afraid something like this would happen". His mother asked, "why do you say that"? My son looked at her and said, "he has been complaining to me and telling me that he didn't know if he should go home after work because he and you haven't been getting along". My wife said to him, "I did not know that he would go to these extremes, but I think we should somehow try to find him". My sons mother asked him, "what do we do, how do we begin". My son replied, "I think that for now we just don't do anything and see if he might come back". "The law will not do anything for at least two or three days anyway". She said, "I know that I've been kind of hard on him but I didn't really believe that he would do this". My son said to her, "there is no use playing the blame game, let's just focus on making things right". "We need to let the rest of the family know"." I'll take care of that." Maybe if things get too bad for him out there, he will change his mind and come back".

I continued working there in the bar, stocking inventory and putting away boxes of products that were brought in by vendors. Of course, I cleaned the restrooms, did the sweeping and just kept things in order. One day, I began feeling pain in my lower abdomen. I sort of examined myself and found that I had developed a hernia. Every day it seemed to get a little worse. It protruded more and sometimes I had to push it back in to ease the pain. I told my boss Jake about it and he said, "I think you had better go to the doctor and have him look at it". He recommended a Dr. to me. I made an appointment for the next week. The doctor examined me and recommended that I have surgery soon. I agreed and the Dr. set up an appointment with the surgeon to do the surgery the next week. I subsequently had surgery and it lasted about an hour and I stayed in the hospital the rest of that day. The owner of the bar picked me up at the hospital and took me home. He said to me, "take as long as you need to heal". "Your job will be there when you are ready to come back to work". I thanked him and went into my apartment. Needless to say, I was quite sore for a couple of days. My friend Frank came to see me. We played cards, had a beer and just visited. Frank told me that he was raised on a farm and only went to the eighth grade in school. He came from a large family of four brothers and three sisters. He said they never had much. Frank also told me, that he never married and did not ever have a very high paying job. But I can tell you, that he is a very good person.

As I sat around waiting to go back to work, something occurred to me. My surgery was paid for by my Medicare and supplementary insurance policies. The paperwork would be mailed to my home address. My wife would see that and would then know where I was. I knew then that I had to move on. I like my job and all the friends I made. It was difficult for me to make the decision to leave. I talked to my boss, Jake, at the bar and told him that I had to move on and my reason for doing so. He had been so good to me and also had been a very good friend. I told him, I would finish out the week and would then be heading out. I told my friend Frank about the decision. I can see that it made him very sad, but he understood the situation and wished me the best of luck. A finer friend you could not have. I will be forever grateful to him. I recommended to Jake, my boss at the bar, that he hire Frank to take my place. Jake said he would talk to him.

I left my apartment, somewhat reluctantly, but I knew this had to be done. I headed for the bus station. I had saved up a little money so that this time I didn't have to hitch a ride. I bought a bus ticket and headed for Deming, New Mexico. I had never been in that area, but decided to go there because I thought it would be remote from any place where they would look for me. It was quite a long ride and I had to change buses a couple of times. I finally arrived there, I was completely lost. I walked down the street carrying my small bag and wasn't sure where to go. I was hungry and tired, so I sat down on a bench to get my bearings and decide what to do.

I got up from the bench and started walking toward the downtown section. I looked like a bum with my beard and crumpled clothes. I was walking along the sidewalk. Suddenly a car pulled up alongside. Two or three young men jumped out of the car. They grabbed me and shoved me into the car. I asked, "what's going on here"? "Let me out of this car right now'. One of them said, "Shut up old of man, we will let you out when we get damn good and ready". And "Another word out of you we'll kick the shit out of you". I sat there silently with the fear that this was going to be the end of my life. They drove me out of town and just kept driving. I estimated that we were approximately 40 miles from the city. There was a kind of stench in the car and I figured they were smoking marijuana. Suddenly they stopped, opened the doors and dragged me out of the car.

I thought, well this is it. They threw my bag into the ditch and kicked me out of the car. I thought again, well this is it. They pushed me down into the ditch and as they drove off. I could hear them laughing and one of them hollered, "take that you son of a bitch". I lay there in the ditch for a while to make sure they were gone. Then I got up and looked around, trying to get my bearings. I knew the city was behind me and I was out in this desert type of country. My fear was that they may come back and it was hard telling what they would do. In the distance, I could see car lights coming toward me, so I scrambled out of the ditch and ran back away from the road. I made sure it was a pretty good distance. There were clumps of Mesquite, so I lay down hoping that they could not see me. They stopped the car, got out and began looking for me. I could hear Them talking.

They said, "No sign of him". "Maybe somebody picked him up", the big guy said. "We better get the hell out of here before the cops come". They drove off, squealing their tires and were soon out of sight. I got up and walked back toward the road, feeling somewhat relieved. However I kept looking up and down the road fearing that they may return. I started walking in the direction of the city. I knew that it was going to be a long walk and I was tired and hungry. I walked and walked, not sure how far. After a few miles, I came to an overpass that crossed over the road that I was on. Being pitch-dark, I decided this might be a good place to spend the night I crawled up under the overpass, where it was under the road. I felt that this would be a safe shelter from any weather that might develop. I sat there with the fear that there could be snakes or maybe other animals that would also decide to spend the night there. I slept for a few minutes and then woke up. This went on for the entire night.

I woke up early in the morning and went down onto the road. I started walking towards the city and I just walked and walked. Car after car passed me by, not one of them made any effort to ask if I was all right or if I needed help. I gave up on trying to catch a ride so I just kept walking. I heard a vehicle slowing down behind. A small truck, with a flatbed stopped. The driver asked if I needed a ride. I said, "I sure do and I certainly appreciate your stopping'. The driver said, "before you jump in, let me move some of this junk so you'll have a place to sit." I asked the driver, "you know of any place in Deming where I could stay, like a room or something on that order"? The driver of the truck said, "My name is Windy". I said to him, "my name is Hank and I am very pleased to meet you Windy". Windy said, "getting back to your question about shelters or soup kitchens, there are a lot of places". As we drove down the road, we talked about a lot of things. He asked about where I was from and where I was headed. He said to me, "I've got some livestock". "There are about 20 hogs, five cows all with calf, 100 chickens, three cats and two dogs". "Oh yes, I also have two horses". "My house has two bedrooms". "You're sure welcome to come and stay with me and possibly help me with the chores or whatever else you can see that needs to be done". "Now, before you give me your answer, I'll stop by there"." You can look at the situation and see if this might be of interest to you and also if you like to cook you can help me with chat too".

His acreage is about a quarter of a mile from the road. At first glance, it was quite impressive. Everything was orderly and neat. You could see that he takes great pride in his property. We went into the house and there again everything is neat and clean. It was nothing fancy, but it gave you the feeling that it was comfortable. He showed me the bedroom where I would be staying. There was a TV set and a radio. Windy said, "What do you think of it"? I said to him, "I think it is wonderful and if you can put up with me I certainly would like to give it a try". "Okay", Windy said, "let's get your bag and you can move in". After putting my bag in the bedroom and getting somewhat settled, Windy said, "let's go outside and I'll show you around, when we stepped out of the house, both of his dogs came running right up to us. They were very friendly. I reached down and petted them and I knew right away that I had made a couple of friends. His cats came and rubbed against my pant legs. It was obvious that Windy loves animals. He showed me the chicken house where his hundred chickens were. The cows were not interested, they were busy eating hay. We walked over to the fence and both of his horses came to greet us. They were very friendly and kind of nuzzled against us.

I said to Windy, "As we go, you'll have to show me what you want me to do and I'll be very happy to help you all I can". "Thanks", Windy said, "you know I have lived here alone for quite some time and I think it would be just wonderful to have some company, somebody to talk to and at the same time I'm hoping that this will also be good for you". "I'm sure it will", I replied.

It became routine to get up in the morning and do the chores. Sometimes Windy would let me do all the chores while he stayed and made breakfast. He was a good cook and was always giving me tips about cooking. Then again, we would reverse the situation. He would do the chores while I made breakfast.

Windy and I have mutual interests. We both love sports and sometimes we watch the football and basketball games together on TV. We talk about our past, families and so forth. Windy confessed to me that he had been married for a short time. He said his wife came from a wealthy family and she expected more from Windy then he could do for her. They were married for about six months and mutually decided to go their separate ways. There were no children and Windy never married again. He was not bitter about the situation and feels that his life is going in the right direction for him

One morning, Windy the said to me, "I got a couple of saddles in the barn, how about you and I taking the horses out for a ride"?

It had been many years since I have ridden a horse but I also remember that I really did enjoy riding them when I was younger. I said to Windy, "I think it would be a lot of fun". We saddled the horses and they were quite frisky and you could tell they had not been ridden for quite some time. We rode them down to the end of the lane and turned around. We gave them their heads and they gave us quite a ride. We rode them about a half mile south of his place. There was a river there, so we rode alongside the river for several miles. We turned around and headed back home. We enjoyed that so much that we decided we would ride them again soon.

When I got up the next morning I could sure tell that I had not been on a horse for some time. My legs and butt were quite sore. Windy was also sore. Again, we thought we wouldn't wait so long to ride again.

Wendy and I would go into town to shop for groceries. We also went to the pool hall, had a couple of beers and played two or three games of pool. I met some of his friends and we had quite a good time visiting. We were standing at the bar I heard someone talking and the voice sounded familiar. I looked down at the end of the bar and there stood the big fella that had abducted me and hauled me into the country. I said to Windy, "that is one of the guys that hauled me out into the desert and dumped me out". I walked up to the big fella and just pushed my way into the Bar beside him. I looked at him and said, "you remember me you bastard"? He looked at me and said, "Who the hell are you"? I said to him, "You and your buddies hauled me out into the desert and dumped me". "That's kidnapping". "Don't move, I'm calling the cops". "The penalty for kidnapping will put you in the clink for several years". "Just stay right there, till the cops get here". He almost ran out of the bar. The rest of the patrons in the bar gave a big cheer and just laughed and laughed. They said to me, "you sure put the fear In that big bastard". "He'll probably never come in here again'.

Once in a while some of Windy's friends would come out to the acreage to visit. Sometimes we would play horseshoe. Windy is quite an accomplished horseshoe player. I had not played for many years, so needless to say, he usually gave me quite a thrashing. Every once in a while I would go out there alone to practice, hoping to compete with him a little better.

I have been there with Windy for about five months and it was so very comfortable there and it felt like home. He went into town one day to take care of some business. He came home and brought a newspaper with him and threw it on the table. I picked it up and started to read through it. In the middle of the paper I saw a picture of myself with these words, "Have you seen this person? If you have, please call this number - - - - - -. I knew then it would only be a short time before someone recognized me. Again, I knew that I had to move on.

I showed the picture to Windy." If I stay here, they would sooner or later find me". "I just don't have any choice". Windy said to me, "I hate to see you go". "You and I have become good friends"." I do understand your situation and I will do everything I can to help you" I told him that I feel very badly about having to leave." You have been such a good friend to me and I really appreciate having the opportunity to know you". "I will miss you, your farm and all the animals".

I packed what few possessions I had and put them in my small bag. I got up early the next morning and went out to the barn. I saddled one of the horses and went for a ride down along the river. I went without Windy because I wanted to be alone and savor my thoughts about all the good times I have had here. When I got back, I took the saddle off the horse and turned it out to pasture. I walked around the ranch and just looked at all of the animals and again thought about how much I will miss this place and Windy.

Windy took me into town in his old truck. On the way we talked about the good times that we had together. We pulled into the bus station and Windy stayed there with me until it was time to board the bus. We shook hands and gave each other a hug. I looked at Windy and saw tears but you know, I also had a tear. It is not often that you are blessed with having a friend as good as he is. He wished me luck and asked that I please keep in touch with him. We waved at each other as the bus pulled out. I will always be thankful to Windy. A better friend you could not have and as he asked, I will keep in touch with him.

My destination was Mesa, Arizona. The bus was full and I got a kick out of the buzz of conversation. There was quite an assortment of ethnic persuasion. An old man was leaning against the window with his eyes shut, never saying a word. A young couple sat just ahead of me. They didn't say much, but they had their arms around each other. There was also a group of young people, possibly a school trip. Just ahead of me in the seat was an older lady. She had white hair along with a kind of bubbly personality. She turned to me and said, "Hello". I responded saying, "How are you"? For the rest of the trip she talked to me about her family and she asked where I was going, where I came from and then continued telling me about her family. Her conversation with me was nonstop, but it did help to pass the time. When we got off the bus, I said to her, "it was a pleasure visiting with you. We shook hands, went our separate ways, never to see each other again.

I left the bus station and began walking down the street, not having any idea of where to go. I was quite hungry so I stopped in a small restaurant. I ordered two eggs, toast and coffee. After breakfast I went out onto the sidewalk and stood there contemplating my next move. I began walking up the street toward the busier part of town. I still had my beard and did look like a bum. I walked by a small park, and noticed there was benches there so I sat down to watch the people walking by. There were all kinds of people, all races and just quite a mixture. Then I saw kind of grumpy looking old man coming down the street. I got up from the bench and when he came near, I walked up to him and said, "I'm not from around here and I need to ask you, do they have any shelters here in this city"? He said, "sure if you just keep walking straight ahead for about 10 blocks you will come to one". "You can't miss it. There's a big sign identifying I have stayed there many times". I thanked him for the information and proceeded to find the shelter. I finally got there and went inside and walked up to the desk. They came over to me and asked, "Can we help you"?

"Yes", I said. "You have a place where I could stay for a couple of days until I get situated"? The lady said, "sure, we do have beds available but you need to be here at least by 9 o'clock to be sure to get a bed". I also asked, "You have a place where I could put my bag"? She motioned and said, "just put it over there on my desk"." I'll take care of it for you". She also told me, "we have food and are open until 7 PM". I thanked her for the help and went out onto the street to begin looking for some kind of employment.

I looked up the street, thinking that I might find a restaurant or bar that could use some help. I went into three or four restaurants and asked if they needed help and I told them that I would be willing to do almost anything. Not much luck there. My appearance probably didn't help. It was getting late so I started walking toward the shelter thinking that a good night's sleep would help and I would get up early in the morning and begin my search for a job. I got back to the shelter in time to have supper. The food was actually pretty good and the bed they gave me was also comfortable. Before going to bed, I sat around talking for a while with some of the guys there. One of them had a real southern drawl with all the Southerners expressions. I'm not ridiculing, just that I like to hear them talk. I imagine my northern accent is also foreign to them. In all of my travels I have found out that there are a lot of good people that are just down on their luck.

Through no fault of their own they are kind of looked down on. Many times, they are not mentally capable or have physical defects. These things are sometimes overlooked when people judge.

There was an older gentleman sitting on the edge of the bed. He had the look of despair about him. I looked at him and decided I would try to talk to him. I said to him, "how are you doing"? He looked at me for a moment and then replied, "I'm alright". I said to him, "my name is Hank and it is nice to see you". He said, "my name is John and I am glad to meet you". I gave him a little rundown on why I am here. Then, he said to me, "I lost my wife about three years ago". "We never had any children and my family is all gone". "My health is not too good and I have very little income so I have to rely on places like this to keep going". "About all I have is my faith in God and I trust that he will be with me and see me through each day". It was quite touching to listen to him. It seemed that he was a very good person and my heart goes out to him and everyone in a similar position. I said to him, "well it was nice meeting you John and I wish you the best of luck:"

I lay down in my bed and began thinking about my family at home. I got to thinking about why my wife was so abusive. I also thought about my family and my conscience bothered me that I was hurting them. Then again, I thought about the abuse and in my own mind my actions were justified. I got up early the next morning and had breakfast. As I went out the door, I said to the lady at the desk, "thank you for the breakfast, it was very good". She said to me, "we are open until 7 PM". I went out into the street and began to search for a job.

Since I had no luck in finding a job at a restaurant, I decided to focus my attention in a different direction. I walked down the street and stopped in several bars to see if they needed help, but I had no luck there either.

I saw a sign chat said. City Hall. I went in there, walked up to the desk where the secretary was sitting. She said, "just sit over there in a chair and someone will be with you shortly". I sat there for quite a while. Then a white-haired older gentleman came out of his office and asked me, "you're the guy looking for work'? I said to him, "yes". He motioned for me to come with him into his office. He said, "Sit down', and also asked my name, age and experience. I told him that I would be willing to do anything and that I had done a lot of hard work in my time. He said to me, "we need someone in the Parks department to do some mowing and just general clean up". The job pays minimum wage and you would be working 25 to 30 hours per week"." We will try you out for about a week to see how you do'.

"You can start tomorrow morning at 8 o'clock". "Before you leave, the secretary will get your Social Security number and any other information that we need". He said, "Good luck and we will see you tomorrow'. I left feeling quite happy and also relieved. My next mission was to see if I could find a place to live, even if I could just find a room that was reasonably priced. I walked down the street thinking to myself, what would be the best way to approach this. As I walked I reasoned that I should probably stop in a real estate office to see if they have any suggestions. After walking several blocks, I finally found a real estate office that advertised that they had rentals available. I went into their office and talked to a lady at the desk. I told her what I was looking for and also told her that I did not have very much money and it needed to be inexpensive. She looked through their files and said that about the only thing they had that would fit my situation was a small apartment above a real retail store. It was up a flight of stairs, nothing fancy, one bedroom, a small kitchen and a small table. The bathroom does have a shower. The rent was quite cheap and after looking at it I decided it would be just fine. I went back to their office and told him that I would take it. It was immediately available so I paid a couple of months' rent, got my meager belongings and moved in.

I went to work the next morning. They immediately sent me out to mow a small park. After mowing the park, I went around and picked up sticks and one not too large limb and put them in a pile. I went back to the maintenance shed and they gave me a pickup truck to go back and load the sticks and limb. They told me where to take them. It was an area where they burn trees and brush. I went back to the maintenance shed to see what else they needed done. The maintenance shed was in a mess so they asked me to rearrange and organize it. The workers had thrown tools and equipment just helter-skelter. After getting it straightened up, the boss came in to tell me that that was enough for the first day and that I could go home. After getting home, I showered, changed clothes and went out and sat on the steps in the front of the building. I just watched the people walking by. A man and his wife stopped. We talked about the weather and I told them that I had just moved into the apartment above. They welcomed me to the neighborhood and said they hoped to see me again. I went up to the apartment, had a sandwich and coffee. I decided to go to bed because I had to get up early the next morning to go to work. As I lay there on the bed I thanked God for all his blessings and for helping me to find a job and a place to live.

I went to work the next morning, looking forward to another good day. The boss called me into his office and said, "good morning". "You did a good job yesterday"." I just wanted to tell you that we did a background check on you". "I see that you are from the Midwest and I am just wondering why you are living here now'? He also asked, "You're not in trouble with the law are you"? I said to him, "no, I am not in trouble with the law, I just had some marital problems and got fed up with it so I took off and decided to live my life in peace". The boss said to me, "those things happen and we wish you the best of luck here". My fellow workers were a happy go lucky group. There was a lot of kidding; joking and they made me feel like one of them. They told me they were going to the bar after work and asked, "Do you want to go with us to have a couple of beers"? I told them, "Sure, I'll go with you". Later when we got to the bar, I could tell that they were regular customers because everyone seemed to know them. We bellied up to the bar and were just enjoying our beer. I enjoyed the camaraderie. A tall mouthy type of person came over to me and said, "Hey old man, think you can handle that"? I didn't answer because I knew he was just looking for an argument. The guys with me said, "just ignore him, he's always looking for trouble". We had a couple of beers and then went home, each in his own direction.

I went to bed that night, with the radio on, listening to music. I got to thinking about my family at home. It bothered my conscience to think that I was putting them through this ordeal of not knowing where their father is. I know they're looking for me and I wish, there was some way of letting them know that I was all right. I don't know if my wife cares or not. I know that I cannot go back to being treated badly again.

Without knowing, my family was frantically trying to find me. My wife asked if they were having any luck finding me. They told her no and they could not tell if she was concerned or not. She asked what method they were using to try to locate me and again, they cannot tell if she was concerned. They were advertising in major newspapers all over the Southwest part of the country. They had some answers to their ads telling them that they thought they had seen me. It seemed that I had managed to always keep a step ahead of them. In my heart I always felt that I would like to be with them but the thought of the treatment I got just wouldn't let me go back.

My working for the city seemed to be going quite well and I began to feel very comfortable there. I was beginning to take on a little more responsibility as time went on and my pay increased considerably. I stayed in my little apartment and began to enjoy more amenities. I even got a little TV set. I am an avid sports fan and enjoy watching baseball, auto racing and in the season, basketball. I did not have a great interest in Pro football, but watching it on TV began to give me more interest. College football and basketball were my favorite sports having played sports in high school.

One evening, I went by myself to the bar that I had gone to with my fellow workers. I stood up at the bar having a beer and talking to a couple of customers. The same guy that had accosted me earlier came up to me and began giving me a hard time. Some of his remarks were quite insulting and he even began to push me. I decided that I had to do something about this or it would get worse. Suddenly, I grabbed him by the throat with one hand and thumb and began squeezing his windpipe. I told him to leave me alone or I would crush his windpipe. He held up his hands in submission to let me know that he was done. I let go and told him" If you ever bother me again, you'll get worse". He never bothered me again. I would see him in the bar but he kept his distance. One of the customers in the bar said, "I don't think I'll ever get you riled". Some of the other guys in the bar remarked, "That's just what he needed". "Maybe he'll leave everybody else alone". I had a couple of beers and decided to go home and watch television. I went to bed and lay there, thinking to myself, I don't know why, but I felt kind of good about my episode at the bar. Maybe he will leave everybody else alone now.

I got up the next morning, showered, shaved and brushed my teeth. I headed for a small restaurant just up the Street from my apartment. I had bacon, eggs, toast and coffee which are my usual. After breakfast I headed for work. It was about six blocks from where I live. After I got to work, I started doing my job having been there long enough to know what was expected of me. A fellow employee and I were sitting at the worksite. We got talking about my family and so forth. They are all grown and they don't know where I am or if I am all right. I thought about calling them, but if I did they would see by the caller ID where I was and I don't want to be found. My friend thought about this for a minute and said, "why don't you call from my cell phone and hope you that you get his answering machine". "You can leave a message and they wouldn't know where you're calling from". He handed me his cell phone and

I dialed my son's number. As I had hoped, I got his answering machine and I left a message saying, "Ron, this is your dad". "I just want you to know that I am all right and that you don't have to worry". "I love you all and miss you'. I hung up and almost had a tear from hearing his voice.

On the way home from work, I stopped at a sporting goods store and bought a pepper spray. I thought this would be some form of protection in case I would be accosted again. It was my hope that I would never have to use it. After leaving the sporting goods store, I went to a large shopping mall to pick up a few items that I needed. I found those items and went to the checkout and while I was standing there, waiting for my turn, someone tapped me on my shoulder. I turned around and it was a man and wife from my hometown. He said, "I thought that was you, but I wasn't sure because you did not have a beard before". Somewhat startled I looked at them and said, "are you on vacation?" Yes", they said, "we have been here for about a week and are leaving for Vegas tomorrow'. "We thought we would try a little gambling since we have never done that before". I said to them. "it was nice to see you but I have to get going". I'm sure that it was on their mind to call home and tell somebody that they had seen me. I knew then that I had to move on.

I sat up that night making plans about where I should go. I knew that it had to be soon. The next morning, I went to work and stopped in the boss's office and told him that I had to leave. He asked me, "is there anything I can do to change your mind"? "No", I said. "Circumstances dictate that I have to leave now". "I just wanted to tell you that I appreciate what you have done for me". I could not have asked for a better boss". We shook hands and I know that he genuinely hated to see me go. We had become good friends. He said, "Hank if you ever get into this area again please come and see me". He also said, "the best of luck to you buddy". I hated to leave and I think we were both teary-eyed.

My plans now are to go to Tucson, Arizona which is about 150 miles South of Mesa. There's an interstate Highway from Mesa to Tucson, so I decided that in order to save some money I would try to catch a ride with a semi-truck. I stopped in a restaurant to get a cup of coffee. There were a couple of truck drivers and I asked if there was a truck stop where I might be able to catch a ride to Tucson. Neither of those two truck drivers we're going in that direction, but they did know where the truck stop was and wished me luck. I walked to the truck stop which was quite some distance away. There were a lot of truckers there and I talked to a couple of them and asked if it was possible to catch a ride. 'They were not too enthused about talking to me, but I kept trying. Then a trucker came over to me and said, "I hear you're looking for a ride to Tucson". I said, "yes I am and I would appreciate catching a ride there". "I'm a little short on funds and it would sure help me". He replied, "we are not supposed to take riders but you look like an alright guy and it would be nice to have company". "I'll be leaving in about an hour, my truck is already loaded and ready to go", "why don't you have a cup coffee and I'll pick you up on the way out'. There was a coffee shop nearby and while I was having my coffee, it was sort of fun to sit there and listen to all those truck drivers talking and, of course, there was the usual truck driver language sprinkled into their conversation.

I sat there drinking my coffee and just listening, minding my own business. With my beard and rumpled clothes and long hair, it was not hard for them to make remarks about my appearance. I am sure they were tempted but they never said anything, even though I did look like a bum. At it had been an hour since the truck driver told me that he would meet me I stood there in front of the coffee shop waiting for the driver to come and pick me up. In just a few minutes he stopped, I climbed in and we were headed for Tucson.

We headed south on the interstate and on our way, he asked me, "Why are you traveling this way"? "You're not in trouble with the law are you"? I explained to him, "I'm not in any trouble but I decided to get away from an unhappy home life". I noticed as we were driving, he kept looking at me which made me feel quite uneasy. Then he said to me, "there is a motel just down the road: we could spend the night there". Now, I really felt uneasy and I realized I was riding with a gay person. I said to him, "you got me all wrong Mr. and when we get to the next town you can stop and let me out". This made him quite angry and he said, "I'll let you out right now you son of a bitch". He put on the brakes and pulled over to the side of the road." Get out now you bastard", he yelled. I was never so happy to get away from a person in my life. So there I was stuck out in the middle of nowhere. I guess my only option was to keep walking toward the next town. I just kept walking and walking until I came to an overpass. I climbed up there just under the road. It was all concrete and I decided to spend the night there. Luckily there were no animals or snakes. I was so very tired and I fell asleep almost immediately and slept most of the night.

I woke up the next morning and climbed down to the road. Actually I felt quite rested and ready to face the day. I started walking down the road toward Tucson. It seemed 100 cars and trucks went by me. I kept walking. I don't know how far and finally a state trooper stopped. He said, "Get in". He began to question me about why I was walking. I explained about my episode with a trucker. 'The trooper said, "I don't blame you". "I'll give you a ride to the nearest town"." I need to ask you, are you in any kind of trouble'? I said. "no, and told him my reason for traveling around. He thought for a moment. "Well I guess it is your right to live your own life". He dropped me off at the nearest town and wished me the best of luck.

It was a very small town but it did have one restaurant and I was terribly hungry. I went in the restaurant, looked around and saw an empty table. I sat down at the table; the waitress came over and took my order. I ordered three eggs, bacon, hash browns, toast and coffee. The waitress must have filled my cup two or three times. I asked the waitress, "how far is it to Tucson"? She answered, "It is about 80 miles from here". I also asked her, "is there a bus that goes through here"? She answered, "yes, but it will be about 4:30 this afternoon when it comes through again." I left her a one dollar tip, and then went to the cashier and paid for my breakfast.

It was about 11 o'clock in the morning and I stood outside the restaurant trying to decide if I should wait for the bus or try my luck at hitchhiking. I decided to walk out to the highway which was about a mile and half away from the restaurant. If I didn't have any luck within an hour I will come back and wait for the bus. I stood alongside the road but nobody would stop for me. Looking like a bum, I'm sure it didn't help. I thought to myself that when I get to Tucson, I would get a haircut and shave and do something about my dirty rumpled looking clothes. It soon became obvious that no one was going to stop to pick me up, so I went back into town and waited for the bus. Some kids walked by me and made a wide swath around me as though they were afraid of me. I guess that was to be expected, more evidence that I needed to clean up my act. I went to the bus station and bought a ticket to Tucson. It was about a half-hour before the bus pulled in so 1 went back to the bench and waited. A police car went by, it slowed down and kind of looked me over but it didn't stop. The bus finally pulled in. I got aboard and waited for departure. It was a short ride to Tucson. I got off the bus and the bus station was quite large. I went into the bathroom to wash my face and hands and then left there, and went out onto the street and began surveying the situation and also began walking. It was getting late in the day. My first thoughts were about finding a place to stay.

I walked several blocks and across the street I saw a sign that said, "SHELTER". 'This was a stroke of luck, finding it so easily. I went into the shelter and asked the man at the desk, "do you have a place where I could stay for the night"? "Yes", he replied, "we have several beds available". I'll take you to one of them". He also said, "if you hurry you can still get something to eat in the dining room". I hurried to the dining room and they were serving soup and sandwiches. This sounded really good to me. I had a bowl of vegetable soup and a ham sandwich. I then went back to the bed that was assigned to me. I put my small bag under the bed. I lay down on the bed and slept through the entire night. The next morning I got up and went back to the dining room where they were serving a smorgasbord type of breakfast. After breakfast, I went back out onto the street and started looking for a place to get a shave and haircut. I stopped someone on the street and asked, "where do I find a barbershop"? He said to me, "just go up the street about four blocks and turn right. go around the corner and you will see their sign". I went into the barbershop and the barber said, "with that beard and your long hair its going to cost you a little extra". I agreed, and he set about cutting my hair and shaving. It took a while because of the extreme growth. When he got done, I looked in the mirror and I sure do look different. I felt almost naked. I told the barber, "I'll just have to get used to it". The barber said, "not a bad looking guy without the beard and long hair". I paid him and left.

My next move was to find some decent clothes. I thought that as long as I was going to buy clothes I might as well dress to fit in with the rest of the people. Now, to find a clothing store. Again, I asked someone in the street, "where do I find a clothing store that sells Western-style clothing"? The person laughed and said, "that's about every clothing store in town". I went down the street and it looked like there were several clothing stores. I walked into the first one that I came to. The salesperson came up to me and asked, "Can I help you"? He also asked, "what type of clothing are you looking for"? I told him, that I needed boots and trousers shirts socks and underwear" we went around the store and I found all of the articles that I needed. I went into a booth and tried them all on and came out looking like a regular south westerner. I looked in the mirror. I thought to myself. "that's not too bad". I asked the man to dispose of my old clothes, which he said he would.

I went out into the street thinking, "Well, I wonder what I can do about finding a job of some kind". I wasn't sure where to start, so 1 thought, I would go get a cup of coffee and do some thinking. This all felt kind of new to me, and about all I needed was a southwestern accent. I spotted a restaurant as I was walking. It looked like a good place to have a cup of coffee. I sat down at the counter. The waitress came over and said, "Hi there, what can I get for you"? I told her that I would have a cup of coffee. "Anything else"? She asked. I replied, "no, this will be all for now". While I was sitting there drinking coffee, a lady came in and sat down beside me. She was kind of attractive, about 60 years old I would guess. She said to me, good morning"." You are new in town here aren't you? She also said to me, "I've never seen you around here before". "I just came here yesterday", I answered. She asked me, "You have relatives or friends here?" No, "I answered". "I'm just vacationing but would be interested in finding work here if here there was something suitable"." What kind of work do you do"? She queried. "Well", I said, "I'm really not that particular as long as it's something that I can handle". She said to me, "I may have something that would be of interest to you". "When we finish our coffee would you like to take a ride with me"? I said, "Yes, what you have in mind"? "I have a job that might be of interest to you". We got in her car and began driving to where the job is located and she also began describing the situation. She said, "I have a small horse ranch about 5 miles out of Tucson". She said, "I am in need of someone to help take care of the horses, do the mowing and all that is entailed in working on a horse ranch". She told me that she has about five horses and they are all Palomino's. "Very interesting", I said. "I will have to find a place to live. I will also need transportation back and forth to your place". "That would be no problem", she said, "I have a small bunk house on the ranch". You can stay there and come to the main house for your meals".

We arrived at her ranch and it was quite impressive. The main house was large and looked to be quite nice. We pulled up to the bunkhouse, got out of the car. "I will let you look at the bunkhouse first to see if that would be suitable". We went inside and looked around. It actually was much nicer than I thought it would be. I told her, "this would be just fine". She then took me to another building where they kept the mowers, pickup truck, wagons and all the equipment needed in the operation. She explained to me what my job would be. I didn't see anything really objectionable and I told her that. She said I can live in the bunkhouse my meals will be furnished and she would pay me $500 a week. I agreed to her terms, She gave me the keys to the pickup which she said was at my disposal. She also said to me, "I know that I don't know you but you seem to be quite a nice person and I think this would work out well for you'. I settled into the bunkhouse and actually was quite comfortable. It had all the amenities, TV set, microwave and quite a nice bathroom. The bunk was all made up with a pillow, sheets and blankets. I thought to myself what more could a guy want. She told me to be at the main house in the morning for breakfast and she would then go with me and show me around the ranch to explain what my job would consist of. Oh by the way", she said, my name is Joan Roth". I said to her, "nice to meet you Joan and my name is Hank Anders".

After breakfast the next morning, we walked around the building site. She showed me everything that had to be mowed and she also said, "we like to keep things looking very neat and orderly". I told her that that's the way I like things and also I would do my best to keep it that way. We went into the horse barn. It seemed that all five of the horses whinnied almost at the same time, sort of friendly and with a feeling that they were glad to see us, She said, "it actually takes quite a bit of work to keep these horses looking nice". I said to her, "I like horses and that will be no problem". She said, "We will open the stable doors and turn the horses out to pasture". "We do that every morning at about this time" "and, obviously, this would be a good time to clean out the stalls".

"We have a bobcat loader and scraper in the storage building that you can use for this". "There are instructions there telling you how much to feed them". "There is a little hay in the loft, which you won't need to feed them since there's plenty of grass"." Well, I'm going back to the house and let you do what you think needs to be done". "Lunch will be ready around 12 noon". "I'll see you then".

As she walked away, I thought, HMMMM, nice boss. I cleaned the stables and hauled it out to the pasture in the manure spreader. I went to the storage building and got out the mower which has a diesel engine that cuts about a 5 foot swath, which would make mowing go pretty fast. I mowed around the buildings. It was such a good mower that it was almost fun to run it. By that time, it was time to go to lunch. I went to the main house and Joan was busy getting lunch ready. I said to her" Joan I hope I'm not too early". She said, "no everything is almost ready". She motioned to me, "there is a bathroom just around the corner there and you can wash up". I came back and sat down at the table. I can see that she had fried chicken, mashed potatoes with gravy, green beans and fresh baked buns, and coffee. I said to her, "do we eat like this every day"? "No", she said, "Since this is your first day, I thought it would be nice to do something special". "It certainly is and I am quite hungry". "Good", she said. I ate dinner and it was so good, I was stuffed. I said to Joan, that was really good but I had better get back to work'. "Oh no", she said, "you and I are going to sit out on the patio and have a cup of coffee and just visit little". We sat there drinking our coffee and Joan said to me, "tell me a little about your family and your life". "We must have sat there for about an hour talking about our families and our lives in general." Joan", I said, "I just have to get back to work". She said to me, "it was fun visiting with you". She also said, "Now don't you go out there and work too hard"." Supper will be at 5:30". "I'll be there", I said as I headed back to work.

Everything went very well there and I really enjoyed working at the ranch. I just love working with horses. It seemed that they were all my friends and sometimes when they were in the pasture I would walk over the fence and they would all come running over to me I would pet them and they would nuzzle against me.

One day Joan came down to the barn and said to me, "that this is such a nice day and I was wondering if you'd like to go riding with me"? I said, "I think that would be a lot of fun". We saddled the horses and headed out. There was a trail that went around a small lake and then past a wooded area. We had been riding for about two and half hours and we decided it was time to get back home. We unsaddled the horses and we both said we would have to do that again sometime. Joan went back to the house. I took care of the horses, wiping them down and currying them. Then I went about finishing my chores.

I was busy one day, cleaning out horse stalls. Joan came into the barn and said, "I'm going to the bar tonight and I thought maybe you would like to go with me". "You can meet some of my friends I think it would be a lot of fun". "Sure", I said, "I really haven't went anyplace for quite a while". I look forward to it. Joan said, "Good, I'll pick you up at about seven". "I'll be ready "I said to her as she walked away.

Joan picked me up and we headed into town. We walked into the bar. I could tell that Joan had been there many times before because all the people said, "Hi Joan", "where have you been"? "Haven't seen you for quite a while"." I've just been kind of busy but I'm here now', she replied. "I'd like you guys to meet Hank". "He works for me at the ranch, so I thought I would bring him along to meet you guys". They all hollered in unison, "nice to meet you Hank". "Likewise", Hank answered.

We sat down at a table with some of Joan's friends and she ordered a margarita for both of us. Her friends, Jeff and his wife Susan, Bob and his wife Betty were all seated there with us. We visited and had such a good time. Joan and I even danced a couple of times and were having fun. At about 11 o'clock, Joan suggested that we head for home. On the way home, we talked and decided we should do this again. I said to Joan, "I like your friends".

We got home at about 1130. I was about to tell her that I would see her tomorrow, but she said to me. "it's not late yet, come in and we will have a drink". We sat down at the kitchen table. Joan poured a drink for both of us. Joan said to me, "excuse me I will be back in a minute". She was gone for about five minutes and came back wearing a slinky almost see-through gown. She sat down at the kitchen table: we talked and had our drinks. She got up from the table and said to me, "come with me". I followed her into the bedroom. She sat down on the edge of the bed and said, "come sit with me". I sat down on the edge of the bed. She took hold of me and pulled me down on the bed with her. I did not expect this and I felt quite uneasy, she grabbed my hand and put it on thigh. Then she took both my hands and held them tight to her breasts. She was quite attractive and it was difficult not to become aroused. She held me close and kissed me. She whispered in my ear, saying, "Please Hank, Please".

The next morning I got up and decided not to go to the main house for breakfast. Instead I just had a cup of coffee and a donut. I went into the barn and decided I would curry the horses. I was in the process of currying one of them when Joan came in. She said to me, "are you mad at me Hank"? "No Joan". "I think it is better that we stay a part for a while". She said, "but Hank, I love you". I said to Joan, "you know I am a married man with a family and it bothers me to break my marriage vows'. "There is nothing wrong with you Joan, you are a very nice attractive lady". "Most anyone would jump at the chance to be with you"." It's just that I do care for my family and if stay here I know what will happen".

"Believe me, I am attracted to you". It has been so nice working here for you and I enjoyed being with you very much but I am going to have to leave". "I will finish out the week hoping chat this will give you time to find someone to replace me". Joan looked at me with tears in her eyes. She did not say a word but just turned and hurriedly walked back to the main house.

I went back to currying the horse and began making plans about leaving. I was unsure about where to go next. 'This has been an ideal situation for me and I just love the work. I really feel bad that I have to hurt Joan but I don't have any choice. I can't decide whether to go to Flagstaff or Yuma. It is still in the middle of the summer and I'm sure would be very hot in Yuma. Flagstaff, being in north-central Arizona, would possibly not be quite so hot I figured that I would take the bus there. Joan came to the barn and said to me, "You're still coming to dinner aren't you"? I replied, "I will be there if you want me to". She looked at me and said, "You know I do".

I went to the main house for dinner. Joan sat down at the table with me and asked, "where will you be going'? "I'm not sure", I replied. "I know I will be taking a bus to wherever I go". She asked me, "would you please let me take you to the bus"? I said to her, "you sure can and I would appreciate that". "I will let you know when". After dinner, I went back to doing my chores. In the middle of the afternoon, Joan came out to where I was working. With tears in her eyes, she said, "would you please reconsider"? "I promise that I won't bother you anymore"." Joan", I said, "you know that if I stay we would soon become involved and I just can't do that". "Sorry, but that is the way it has to be". Again, she went back into the house crying.

After finishing the day's work, I went to the main house and had supper with Joan. I asked her, "have you begun looking for someone to replace me'? "No Hank, I haven't, I'm convinced that that just won't happen, so I will begin looking tomorrow". I said to her, "Joan I know that the right guy will come along and he will be very lucky to have you". "When he does come along be sure you love that person". "Loving each other is the main ingredient in a personal relationship and I certainly do wish you all the happiness possible".

I finished our the week, making sure that I left the place in tip top shape. I packed my meager belongings in a small bag and then walked to the main house to tell Joan that I was ready to leave. "You did tell me that you want to take me to the bus didn't you"? "Oh yes, of course, I'll be with you in just a minute" she was dressed in a suit and heels. Her blondish hair was to perfection. I thought to myself, she is a very attractive woman. We got into the car and headed to the bus station. I thanked her for all that she did for me and I wished her the best. When we got to the bus station, she got out of the car and went with me to buy my ticket to Flagstaff. There would be a transfer at Mesa to another bus from Mesa to Flagstaff. They announced that the bus was loading. She walked with me to the bus and just before I got in, she whispered in my ear "I love you". I did not know how to respond to that but I did tell her goodbye and that I hope everything will go well for her. She said to me, "well take care of yourself and I hope to see you again sometime'. I got on the bus and as we left, I thought to myself that this was probably the last time I would see her.

We left the bus station and headed north toward Mesa. The bus was full and you could hear the buzz of conversation. I sat next to an older gentleman. He looked at me and said, "My name is Tom". I'm headed for Mesa'. I said to him" my name is Hank" I'm on my way to Flagstaff". He was a World War II veteran, like me, so we exchanged war stories and actually it was quite enjoyable talking with him. As we were traveling, I suddenly had a kind of sharp pain on my right side and it was more toward my back. It went away and I thought no more of it. I looked out the window, kind of enjoying the scenery I dozed off and slept for about a half hour. Tom said, "don't be surprised if I do the same". By the way, Tom said, "I'm retired and have been for some time".

"Lost my wife a couple of years ago, and have just been kind of floating around since". He also said, "never had any kids and I really don't have any ties anyplace". I told Tom, "I am still married and have kids". "I left my wife a few months ago'. "My kids, by the way are, all grown married and have kids". "My wife got so abusive that I just couldn't live with it anymore and I have just been knocking around since". "I am headed for Flagstaff and I really don't know for sure what I'll do there or what my plans are". We enjoyed talking with each other, but I did find out that we were worlds apart politically, so we kind of stayed away from any discussions concerning politics. We reach Mesa and as the bus was pulling into the station, I said to Tom, "it's been a pleasure visiting with you and I hope everything goes well for you". Tom said, "thank you and you have a good trip". I got off the bus. It was about an hour before the other bus will leave for Flagstaff. I found a coffee shop and decided to have a cup of coffee and maybe a donut. After having coffee, I found a bench in the bus station and just sat there watching people. I noticed how many obese people there are, not only older people, there was some a young people that are quite obese. You see people on crutches, some were walking with canes, there were quite a few with walkers and many people were quite bent over. It makes you realize how lucky you are to be in good health. It was time to get on the bus and head for Flagstaff. I kind of felt like I was starting on a new adventure.

The bus to Flagstaff was quite interesting. The scenery was impressive, lots of trees and mountains in the background. Some of the land was quite barren. All in all it was nice and actually very inviting as we were heading toward Flagstaff, I sat there in the bus pondering my future. My first move was to find a place to stay and secondly, a job of some kind.

We pulled into the bus station at Flagstaff. After getting off the bus I retrieved my bag and walked out onto the sidewalk. There was city in either direction, which way should I go? I started out walking not knowing where I was going. I had saved up some money in my last job so if necessary I could spend the night in a hotel or motel. As I was walking I saw a small restaurant. I said to myself, "guess I'll just go in there and get something to eat and maybe figure out what next move should be. I went in and sat down in a booth. The waitress came over and I ordered, from the menu, chicken fried steak. She brought coffee to me and almost immediately brought my order. 'The steak was smothered in white pepper gravy and was it ever good. Afterwards, I just sat there sipping my coffee. The waitress came over and asked, "can we get anything else for you"? "No thank you", I replied. I left a tip for the waitress and paid the cashier. Before I left I asked, "you know if they have a shelter here in Flagstaff"? She said to me, "there may be but I would not have the slightest idea where it could be". I said to her, "thanks for the help". I left the restaurant and started walking down the street. Suddenly I felt a very sharp pain in my right side and also kind of toward my back. I had experienced a similar pain on the bus trip here; however this one was more severe and did not go away. I sat down on the edge of the curb, sweating profusely and I was beginning to panic. What should I do, the pain became so severe that I was beginning to groan. A passerby heard me and came over and asked, "are you all right"? I said to her, "no I have a terrible pain"." I need some help". She immediately got out her cell phone and dialed 911, She stayed there with me until an ambulance arrived.

They put me in the ambulance and took me to the emergency room at a nearby hospital. The doctor examined me and said, "I think it is your gallbladder". "We will do some further testing"." Sit tight, we will get back to you shortly". In just a few minutes, he came back and said, "it is your gallbladder and we will do surgery immediately. If you haven't had your appendix out we will take care of that also".

They, of course. came around questioning me about insurance and my means of paying. I gave them my Medicare card and also my supplementary insurance card. They told me that I am well covered. They also brought the clip board with a sheet for me to fill out. I told them, that I was absolutely not able to fill it out at this time. They said they would do that for me and began asking questions and address, age, previous surgeries and all of the usual information that they require. I answered their questions as best I could. Considering the circumstances. They prepped me and wheeled me into surgery. I woke up in the recovery room, where they kept me for about an hour, and then took me to my room. A short time later the Dr. stopped in and told me that the surgery was very successful and that I would probably stay in the hospital for about three days.

The hospital room that I was in has two beds. The other bed was occupied by an older gentleman. He told me he was there because he had a hernia operation and that he also would be there for three days. He said to me, "my name is Fred Landon", to which I replied, "Nice to meet you Fred", my name is Hank".

I also told him that I had just had gallbladder surgery and would be in the hospital for about three days. He told me that he lives right here in Flagstaff and has his own business which is a small bakery. I told him, "first job I ever had was in a small town bakery". "Tell me", Fred asked, "you live here in Flagstaff'? | told him, "no", and that I had just arrived here in Flagstaff I said to him, "as soon as I get out of the hospital, I will begin searching for a job and a place to live".

Fred told me he had lost his wife about five years ago. She died from a brain tumor. It is just him alone since they never had any children. I cold him that I left home because I just could not stand cruelty any longer. Fred said to me, "sometimes you do what you gotta do". Fred is an avid sports enthusiast, which we certainly had in common. Fred left the hospital the day before me. Before he left he said to me, "Hank, when you when get released, stop in Landon's Bakery". "I want to talk to you". He gave me the address and said, "please don't forget to stop in and see me". Before the hospital released me they asked me to stop in the business office to give them the information they need to complete their paperwork. I told them, "I am just new in town and do not currently have an address". "As soon as I get situated, I will stop in and give you my new address". They said that would be just fine.

The next day I left the hospital not having any idea where Landon's bakery is. Luckily a cab had just let somebody out at the hospital. I flagged the cab down and had the driver take me downtown to Landon's Bakery.

I walked into the bakery and up to the counter where a young lady had been waiting on customers. She asked me, "Can I help you"? I said, "yes, I'm here to see Fred". She hollered into the back room, "Fred you have a visitor". Fred came and smiled as soon as he saw me. He said, "Hank, come on back and I'll show the place to you". Fred looked like a Baker with a tall white hat and his white apron. Fred said "the reason I asked you to come here is because I have an idea that I want to run by you and see what you think about it". "As you can see, I work here alone and I am so tied down, I cart even go get a cup of coffee". "Would you be interested in coming to work for me"? "Before you answer, let me tell you about the job". "First, there is a little two room apartment above the store, its nothing fancy but clean and there is everything there that you need". "There is even a TV set, a radio and a microwave'. "You could live there and it wouldn't cost you anything except that I want you to work for me in the bakery"." I don't have a job description, but to be begin with, you would be doing odd jobs around the bakery, some cleaning and even at times waiting on customers at the counter'. "As we go I will involve you more and more in the baking". "To start with I will pay you minimum-wage, which would increase as you take on more responsibilities'. "If you take the job, I'll give you the keys and you can move in immediately". I could feel a wave of happiness all over me because this would be so ideal. I said to Fred, "thank you my friend, this is ideal for me and I certainly will work for you". He handed me the keys and said, "be here at 6 AM and we will go from there".

The next morning I promptly walked into the bakery at 6 AM. Fred said, "good morning Hank, the coffee is on and the eggs are frying'. "Toast is in the toaster'. "There is a little breakfast nook over there". "Dishes and silverware are in those cupboards over there also". "I'll let you finish the eggs and toast". I did as he asked and he and I sat down together and had our breakfast. While we were eating, he told me what he would like to have me do. After breakfast he gave me an apron and a tall white hat. Fred laughed and said, "Now you look like a Baker". With a smile, I said, "I guess I do". Fred said, "there is a dumpster out in the back, where you can empty the garbage out there". In the meantime, Jennifer, who works out front at the counter came in. Fred said, "Jennifer this is Hank, who is going to be working here". Fred said, "pay attention to her, she is a very good worker and is so good with the customers". Jennifer said to me, "every morning we deliver four dozen donuts to the convenience store which is about eight blocks down the street. She said to me, "you occasionally will have to do that when I'm not here".

Fred showed me how to slice the bread, package and label it. We had three different varieties of buns which he also showed me how to package. "We do make pies, but only when ordered". "You'll learn about all these things as we go". "Now, I come to work, at 3 AM every morning and after you've been here for a couple of weeks, I probably will have you come in earlier." The good part of that is, that we also go home in the middle of the afternoon, this will give you time to do a lot of other things".

I enjoyed working for Fred. He is so easy-going and has quite a jolly personality. We kid each other a lot, creating a relaxed atmosphere that's not to say that we don't take the work seriously, because Fred is a stickler for quality and aims for a top-notch product. I had been working for Fred for about three weeks we got done working about 3 o'clock that afternoon. I left the store and began walking down the street. I heard a car honk. I didn't really pay any attention, just kind of glanced around. I kept walking and the car honked again. I turned around and looked. I cannot believe my eyes. There was Joan sitting in her car, smiling at me. I walked over to her car, and said, "what in the world are you doing here Joan "? She said, "Hank, I just had to see you". I got in her car. She reached for me and kissed me. "Hank", she said, "I know that you don' like this I just can't help myself". "I know nothing can come of this, but if I could just see you once in a while, I'll settle for that". I said to her, "Joan, I am very glad to see you". She asked me, "how are you doing, truthfully"? "Is everything going all right for you"? I told her about my job in the bakery and also I told her about my boss Fred, who is such a good guy and that I am very happy with my situation here. We drove to a restaurant and had supper together and had a long conversation. I do know that she cares for me and I told her again that I was a married man with a family. She said she understood and wished me the very best. She gave me her phone number and asked me to call her if I ever needed her. I promised her that I would. She took me back to my apartment and left on her trip back home. Before she left, I asked her, "how in the world did you find me"? Joan said, "I knew that you had to come here to Flagstaff". "I didn't have any idea where you were but I just took a chance and parked along the street hoping that you would come by". "You don't know how happy I am to have found you". She also didn't know how happy I was to see her.

I went to bed that night and laid there thinking about my family and a feeling of loneliness crept over me. I cannot help thinking that they were all quite angry with me for putting them through this. I've been gone for several months and I hope they have adjusted. I lay there with all kinds of thoughts going through my mind. I finally fell asleep and woke up at about 4:30 in the morning. I showered, brushed my teeth got dressed and headed to work.

Fred was already there and had the bread ready to be put in the oven. I put the bread in the oven and set the timer. Fred said, "the griddle should be hot". "I have the pancake batter all mixed". "You can make pancakes for me and however many you want". "In the bottom drawer of the refrigerator you will find bacon". "Make a couple of strips for me and however many you want". "The coffee is already made". We sat down and enjoyed our breakfast also discussing what we needed to bake for that day.

The store was quite busy that day so I had to help at the counter, taking care of customers, taking orders and refilling the case. I had had some experience working in a bakery, when I was younger. I suggested to Fred that he order frozen cookies. That way he could have a larger variety, and we would not have to stock ingredients or mix the dough. "I've had customers ask for macadamia nut cookies and also coconut pecan cookies". Fred said, "You're probably right, but let me give that some thought".

Later that day, as we were getting ready to go home, Fred asked me, "you like to fish"? I answered, "I sure do, why do you ask"? Fred said, "I have been thinking about going up north to the Colorado River". "They say it is good fishing up there this time of the year". "I thought we could get up early Saturday morning and have all the work done in the bakery by noon". "We can get up there and camp overnight and fish all day Sunday". "I can get the pickup camper ready and I think it would be a lot of fun". I told Fred, "I don't have any fishing gear or a fishing license" Fred said. "I have all kinds of fishing gear and when you get done here today, run over to the courthouse and pick up a license". I did as Fred suggested. Fred said, "we can probably get in some fishing that night". "Also we can buy bait when we get there'. Fred said, "Let's plan on being here at about 3 o'clock in the morning so we can be done by noon and out of here and on our way north to the river".

We both met at three in the morning and immediately mixed all the dough. We hurried around so that we could get everything done by noon, which we did. Fred told Jennifer to put the money in the safe." We can bank it Monday morning". As we walked out the door, Fred said to Jennifer, "well Jennifer, you're the boss, see you Monday". Finally we're ready to go. We got into the pickup and Fred said, "We're off".

We headed north to the river and got there at about 8 o'clock in the evening. We found a camping spot right along the river and immediately got out our fishing equipment. There was a bait shop not too far away so we walked there and bought our bait. We decided to use live bait, so we bought a variety of sizes, from minnows to chubs an even larger. Fred cast his bait out into the current and almost immediately caught about a 25 inch northern pike. I cast my bait into a quiet water area, using a plain minnow. I had a bite and caught a really nice sized bass. We fished for about three hours and both caught several fish. Fred said, "I'm kind of tired, let's call it a day and get up early in the morning and start again. "Sounds good to me", I said. We put the bait in a large cooler in order to keep them overnight.

We had brought some cold meat and bread with us. That was our supper and, of course, we had a couple of beers along with that. The bunk beds were quite comfortable and we both slept very well that night. When I woke up, Fred was already cleaning the fish that we caught the night before. He told me, "I thought some good old pan fried fish would taste pretty good this morning". I agreed with him and immediately helped prepare our breakfast. That was probably the best tasting fish I ever had. I said to Fred, "you're a darn good cook". Fred looked at me with that grin of his and said, "Well, I've had a little experience".

After breakfast, we went to the river and fished until noon. We both had several good catches. We went to the camper and cleaned the fish and then it was back to the river and I fished again while Fred took the camper to see if he could find some dry ice to put in the cooler with the fish that we cleaned. I caught a couple of really nice ones while he was gone. Fred came back with the dry ice, put it in the cooler along with the fish that we had cleaned. He motioned for me to come to the camper and he handed me a couple of burgers. We ate the burgers along with a beer and afterwards went back to our fishing. We fished until about 4 o'clock in the afternoon and took our catch back to the camper. We cleaned our fish, put them in the cooler, gathered up our gear and headed back toward Flagstaff. We stopped in a restaurant on the way back and had a steak. It was about 11 o'clock when we got back to Flagstaff. Fred dropped me off at my apartment and said, "I'll unload everything". "One of these days well have a fish fry". I said, "good night, see you in the morning".

I walked into the bakery the next morning. Fred was there mixing up the dough and buns that we would bake for the day." Hank', he said. "we got our boxes of frozen cookies". "Why don't you put some on pans and bake them to see how they turn out". I filled two pans and put them in the oven. We baked, as per instructions. We took them out of the oven and they looked just great. Of course, we had tasted them and they were very good. Fred said, "Why don't you package about five dozen and put them out in the case to see how they sell"? We will start them out at $2.99 a dozen and will see if you have a good idea here". We put them in the case with a sign saying NEW PRODUCT". By midmorning they were all gone. Fred said, "it looks like you came up with a great idea Hank". I replied, "thank you'.

I really like working with Fred. He and I get along really well. We spent a lot of time joking and of course swapping war stories. We were both World War II veterans, he was in the Army and I was in the Navy. We also both like sports and a couple of times we went to a basketball game at a local high school.

One day at work, Fred said. "I've got to be gone on some personal business fora couple of days'. "You know what has to be done so I'll just turn it over to you." Run it just like it's yours". "I'll let Jennifer know that you are the boss and all decisions that need to be done, will be up to you". "You will get along with Jennifer; she has been a great employee".

I ran the bakery while Fred was gone. Everything went well and there were no problems. The third morning I went to work early and expected Fred to be there. I walked into the bakery.

Fred was not there which was quite unusual. I thought possibly that his business could be taking longer than he thought. Then again, I'm just sure that Fred would've called us if he was going to be gone longer than he thought. I called his home, but there was no answer. As the day wore on, I became more worried since he did not answer his phone and also the fact that he did not contact us. I got the baking done for the day bur still no word from Fred. I told Jennifer about my concern and she agreed that Fred certainly would have let us know. I said, "Jennifer I'm going over to Fred's house just to check in and see if he might be there". I drove across town to where Fred lives. I knocked on the door, but there was no answer. I tried the door; it was not locked, so I walked in. I went through the living room and into the kitchen and there was Fred lying on the floor. I called to him saying, "Fred, are you all right"? There was no answer. I felt his face and it was cool. I got no pulse and I was quite sure that he was dead. I called 911, giving them the address. Soon, a police car and an ambulance pulled up. I opened the door for them and told them that he was in the kitchen and I was quite sure that he was not alive. The ambulance people told the police. It appears that he must have suffered a heart attack. The police wanted to know how I fit into the picture and I explained to them that I was an employee who has been running the bakery for a couple of days while Fred was gone on business. I also told them that he had not showed up at work which was very unusual and I had tried all day long to contact him. I finally got worried and went to his home to check on him. The police asked me if I knew what funeral home he should be taken to and I told them, "no, I have no idea". "He has no family that I know of and he has never discussed this with me".

I told the police that I am not sure what I should do next but I would go to the bakery and make sure everything was shut down and I would put a sign on the door saying CLOSED UNTIL FURTHER NOTICE. I went back to the bakery and broke the news to Jennifer. She was shocked. She had worked for Fred for several years and I know this was a terrible blow to her.

I said to Jennifer, "it has been your job all these years to pay the bills"" The vendors, utility bills, the paychecks, and so forth would need to be paid, please continue to do this until things get settled".

The police notified me that they had gone through Fred's house and found his checkbook and financial records. They also found his will and turned it over to Fred's lawyer, whose name address and telephone numbers were amongst his papers. They asked if I would stay on for a few days to help get the business ready for sale. I agreed to do that and said to Jennifer, "you should also stay on since you are the financial Sec.". They said this would be fine but to be sure to keep the records for the attorney.

I was busy doing some cleaning in the bakery, Jennifer called me into the office and said to me, "I know that you have not been paid for about three weeks, so I will make out a check to you for what you have coming and also I will give you a separate check in the amount of $1000". Fred discussed that with me a few days ago because he thought you deserved a bonus." You will be paid for every day that you are here until the job gets done".

Jennifer asked if I would go with her to the funeral Chapel the day of Fred's funeral. They could not find that Fred had any religious connections. We were sitting there during the funeral and I was listening to the minister's sermon. It suddenly hit me, that in all my travels I have not been paying any attention to God. I will do so from now on.

The next day, the lawyer came into the bakery. He said, "we have looked at Fred's will and he has left the bulk of his estate to a children's home here in town". "Jennifer" he said, "Fred left you the sum of $25,000". A surprised Jennifer said, "I will always be grateful to him for that". Jennifer told the attorney about the bonus that she was going to give me because Fred had talked about doing that. The lawyer said, "that is perfectly all right as long as there are funds in his bakery account to cover it". Jennifer assured him that there was. Before the lawyer left, he said, "both of you are doing an excellent job and we hope that you will continue until everything is settled". We told him that we would.

I continued to come to work in the bakery every day, making sure that all of the perishable ingredients were taken care of and that the gas lines into the oven and furnace were turned off. It took about three days to get everything done. I then went to Jennifer and told her that I had done everything that needed to be done. She said to me, "there will be no hurry about you moving out of the apartment'. "I'm sure it will take some time to sell the bakery". I thanked her and said, "there will really be no purpose in my staying, so I will be moving on". I wish you the best of luck." Jennifer said, "we hate to see you go and it certainly has been a pleasure working with you and I wish you the best of luck".

Jennifer handed me my paycheck and also the bonus check. I went to the apartment and packed the few belongings that I had. I decided to leave them in the apartment and go to the bus station to see when the bus would leave for Kingman, The next bus to leave for there would be at 9 o'clock the next morning. On the way back to the apartment, I stopped in the restaurant and had one of my favorites, chicken fried steak with pepper gravy. After finishing supper, I went back to the apartment, actually feeling kind of lonely. I missed Fred and all the laughter he and I had together. I turned on the TV and watched a couple of programs and the news. I lay down and went to sleep and slept through the whole night. I woke up at

5:30 AM. On the way to the bus station, I stopped in a small diner and had some breakfast. I got to the bus station at about 830 and just sat there on the bench until it was time to board the bus. I bought a newspaper, having not looked at a paper for quite some time and it was interesting to see what was happening in the world.

I boarded the bus for Kingman. It was not crowded. I sat together with a tall slim cowboy looking sort of guy. He also was headed for Kingman where he was going to pick up a truck. He was starting a new job, working for a trucking company and was taking a load to San Francisco. He said, "if you don't have anything going on, you can ride out there with me". "No thanks", I said." the last trucker that I rode with turned out to be gay and I don't want any part of that". He laughed, and said, "I'm as straight as you can be. I like women too much to be that way". I answered, "me too". I got to thinking; I wish I would have called Joan.

As we were riding on the bus, I went to sleep. I must've slept for at least an hour. The fellow next to me, kind of laughed when I woke up. He said, "man you can snore". Kiddingly, I said to him, "didn't bother me any". We both laughed. We hit the outskirts of Kingman and I just kind of looked around to see what the town is like. It looks like almost any other town except it did have a kind of inviting appearance. We pulled into the bus stations I got my bag and went outside onto the street. I just looked around, and I thought, you know I just don't have the slightest idea what my next move should be. Since I have some money, I thought I would find a motel and spend a couple of nights there, giving me time to think about what my

Next move should be. A couple of people were standing there and I asked them, "Where do I find a motel"? They said to me, "if you just keep walking straight ahead on this street for about a half a mile you will come to a motel on the left side of the street". I walked in the direction that they told me, and just as they said, there was a motel. I went in and registered for two nights. There was a telephone in the room, so I thought I would call Joan. She had given me her number and she had asked that I call her. The phone rang a couple of times and when she answered I said, "Joan this is Hank". She said, "Oh Hank, it is so good to hear your voice" Where are you"? I told her, "I am in Kingman Arizona". "I just got here a little while ago and I am registered in the motel." "I will stay here in the motel the next couple of nights until I get situated". Joan said, "why didn't you come down here"? I told her, "Joan I would like to, but I'm still a married man with family". She asked me, "would you care if I come to Kingman and spend a couple of hours with you'? I replied to her, "why don't you wait until I get situated?" It will be a couple of days before I know for sure what I will do and I will call you then". She said, "okay, I will be waiting for your call".

I woke up the next morning feeling quite rested. I showered and shaved so that I would look presentable when I went job hunting. Having just worked in a bakery, I thought I would look around and see if they have a bakery here in Kingman, first I stopped in the restaurant to have some breakfast. I sat down at the counter and the waitress came over and took my order. There was a gentleman sitting beside me and I said to him, "excuse me, I am new in town here". "Do you know if there is a bakery here in Kingman"? "Well, actually there are two", he replied. "One is a larger commercial type and the other is more of a family type". He also said, "the family type bakery is located about four blocks from here." To get there, just go 3.blocks down the street, and then turn right". It will be about a half a block from the corner". You can't miss it"." The name of it is, THE CITY BAKERY". I thanked him and said, "I appreciate your help". He replied, "glad I can help you".

I finished my breakfast and paid the check. I proceeded to find the bakery. The Instructions he gave me were right on. I walked into the bakery and the girl at the counter asked, "how can I help you"? I said, "I would like to see the manager please"." Just a minute", she said and went into the back room. A man came out and if you have ever pictured a Baker in your mind, this fella surely fits that description. He was rather short on the heavy side and had on his white bakers clothing, a Baker's hat and a very pleasant grin. He said to me, "what can I do for you"? I told him that I was looking for a job. "I don't know", he said. "Have you had any experience"? I replied, "yes I have". "I worked in the Landon bakery in Flagstaff'. "Why did you leave there"? He asked. I told him that the owner had suddenly died from a heart attack." "They closed the bakery and I did not know if they would continue to operate it". The Baker said to me, "I'm sorry to hear that. I wasn't aware that Fred had passed on".

"What did you do there? I said to him, "I did almost everything, including baking"." Well", he said, "why don't you come here about 8 o'clock in the morning and we will see what I can find for you to do". "I have an older gentleman that has been working with me for several years and I think he will soon retire, so I probably will need someone quite soon". I thanked him and said, "I will see you in the morning at eight". I left the bakery feeling quite happy. 'This is just what I need.

I went back to the motel thinking that I would take a little rest before I started looking for a place to live. But then, I remembered that I had promised Joan that I would call her. I dialed her number and it rang several times. Finally, she answered. I said to her, "Joan this is Hank?". "I'm calling you as I promised". "I'm here in Kingman and I got a job working in the city bakery". Joan said, "oh it so good to hear from you"." I think about you all the time". "Can I come there to see you? I told her, "sure as long as you understand that I'm still a married man with a family". She said, "Sure, I understand". I told her that when she gets here, just stop in the city bakery and ask for me. She replied, "I'll see you in a couple of days".

In the afternoon I looked for a real estate business that also handled rental properties. I thought I would just wall around the city to see what I can find and also to acquaint myself with the city. It appeared to be a bustling city, neat and also attractive. As I was walking, I stopped and asked a gentleman about where I can find a place that handles rental properties. He told me that actually there were several, but there was one just up the street. I thanked him, and walked up the street and into the real estate office. The lady at the desk looked up and asked, "what can we do for you? I told her that I was looking for a small apartment that was not too expensive. There were several options but most of them were too expensive. I thanked her and went out the door and proceeded to find another real estate office. I found one and went into their office and told them my situation and also told them that I cannot afford anything very expensive. She said. "We do have a place that offers rooms for rent'." It's an older house but the rooms are nice and clean". "We will take you there and you can see for yourself whether or not it would fit your needs". We drove to the house and I looked around. They had a room available on the first floor that has its own bathroom. The rent was in the range that I could afford. It was about 10 blocks from the bakery.

I guess, walking the 10 blocks to the bakery would be good exercise for me. I said to the real estate people, "looks good to me, I'll take it". It was available immediately so I paid a couple months' rent in advance. It was quite a distance to the motel where I was staying, so I took a cab to there. I picked up my bag and took it back to my apartment. I unlocked the door a put my bag just inside the door and then locked it again. I then looked for a place to eat. There was a small diner about three blocks from my room. I guess I lucked out there. After eating,

I walked back to my room and sat down to read a newspaper that I had just picked up while at the diner. I read for a while and then decided to go to bed so I could get rested for my first day of work at the bakery.

The next morning I walked into the bakery at 8 o'clock. The boss said, "good morning and by the way my name is Pete". I said, "good morning Pete, my name is Hank". I could tell right away that I would enjoy working for Pete. His assistant was working at the table where they made the various pastries and breads. Pete said, "Jens, this is Hank". He will be working with us and I would appreciate your teaching him what you do here". Jens said, "sure I'll be glad to do whatever I can and it is a pleasure to meet you Hank". They made and sold lots of Danish pastries and cookies. They made the usual variety of breads, pumpernickel rye, Marble rye, wheat bread, Italian bread and white bread. They also make cakes and wedding cakes that are ordered by 7 customers. A lady comes in two days a week to decorate them.

I was working one day when Helen, the lady that works at the front counter came back and said there is a lady out here to see you. I said to her, "thank you Helen, tell her I'll be there in a minute". I went out front and there was Joan. I said to her, "I didn't expect to see you this soon.

Joan said, "I came as soon as I could, I was so anxious to see you". I said, "Joan I get off work in about an hour and a half and I'll meet you out front". "I'll be waiting for you", Joan said. I went back into the bakery, Pete said, "girlfriend?" Not exactly", I said." I have known her for a while and we have become good friends". Pete smiled and said, "Sure, that's where it starts".

When I got off work, I went outside from the bakery and Joan was sitting there waiting for me in her car. I got in with her and she leaned over and kissed me. I know I shouldn't have, but I kissed her back. I asked Joan, "how long do you plan to stay? Kiddingly she said, "as long as you will let me". Then she said to me. "I would like to stay overnight and then go back home tomorrow". I said to Joan, "Let's drive around town just to see what it's like". Joan said, "Sounds Like a plan to me". We drove around looking at the sites and I told her about my job at the bakery. She said to me, "why don't you just come home with me? I responded saying" you know I would like to be with you". She said. "I do understand and I guess we will have to live for the moment".

We drove around, looking the town over. And Joan said, "That looks like a nice restaurant across the street"." I'm starving". "Let's go there and have something to cat"." Looks good to me', I said. We sat there eating and talking and I thought to myself, "I could easily fall in love with Joan, she is a wonderful person and I truly believe that she loves me".

We left the restaurant. Joan said to me, "I had better find a place to stay". I said to her, "the motel that I stayed in for a couple of nights is not too far from here and it is quite nice". We drove to the motel and I waited in the car while she went in to register. She came out and said, "my room number is 112". "Will you help me carry my bags in'? "Of course", I said. We took her things in and she said, "Why don't you stay and watch TV with me for a while"? "Sure, I haven't watched TV for a few days." She said, "we can just lay on the bed and watch, it would be more comfortable". We lay there watching T'V. Joan put her arms around me and said, "I want you Hank". "Please Hank, please" Suddenly I woke up. It was 7 o'clock in the morning and I had to be to work at eight. I woke Joan and said to her, "I have to be to work at eight".

She said, "They have a complimentary breakfast here, let's go there, have breakfast and Ill take you to work". Joan asked, "why don't you see if you can take an hour off for lunch"? "We can go someplace and have lunch and afterwards I had better head for home'. I said to Pete, "Joan is going home today and wants me to have lunch with her before she leaves, so would it be all right if I took an hour for lunch"? He said, "no problem, you guys enjoy your lunch". Joan picked me up at noon; we went to a restaurant and had lunch while we visited. Afterwards, we got in her car and she reached over and kissed me and said, "I love you". I responded by giving her a big hug. She dropped me off at the bakery and left for home. I watched her drive away. It left me with an empty feeling. Before she left, she asked me to please keep in touch with her. I promised that I would.

I went back to work in the bakery. Jens said to me, "I'll be making some Danish and I'll show you how we form them". I watched him and it was quite similar to what we had done in other bakeries that I had worked in. The phone rang and Jens asked me to answer. I answered, "City bakery, may I help you"? It was a lady calling to order a cake. I got an order form and took her order this was old hat for me since I had done it many times before. I was getting more involved in the operation of the bakery every day. Having worked in other bakeries, I have developed quite an interest in that business. Before I went home that day, the boss took me aside and said, "I'm very happy with your work here". "You fit in good and it's a pleasure to work with you"." You know Hank; I hired you with no questions asked". "You look to be a clean-cut decent person so I just went ahead and hired you".

"Okay I guess I have gotten a little curious and wondering why you are here". "You care if I ask those questions now"? "No, certainly not". "I will tell you that I am not wanted by the law and I am here of my own choice". "I am here because I lived in a mean atmosphere where I was continuously being picked on. This went on for years. It got to the point where I couldn't take it any longer, so I left not telling anyone were I was going and I have not had contact with them in almost a year, with one exception." "I do have four grown children and I did get a message to the oldest son telling him that I was okay and that I miss them. I did not actually talk to him. I left a message on his answering machine." "So here I am trying to make a new life for myself." He said to me "that's interesting and that is all I need to know."

"You certainly do well and hope you are happy here." "You can stay as long as you like." It is actually a lot of fun to meet people and make more friends. Once in a while Jens and 1 would stop in a bar and have a couple of beers. We became friends with some of the customers. And just had a lot of fun just talking about sports, news happenings, and very little politics. Jens was also single, having lost his wife some years ago.

Jens and I were talking one day and he said to me, "I have an idea that I will run by you and see what you think". "We get off at about 1 o clock Saturday afternoon". "How about if you and I drive to Vegas and do a little gambling and maybe take in a show? Jens also said, "Ill drive my car, it is not so terribly far". I thought for a minute and replied, "that sounds like a lot of fun, let's go for it." So Saturday afternoon after work, Jens and I headed for Vegas. We had a little time before going to the show that we wanted to see, so we did a little gambling, mostly on the slots. We went to a show and it was very enjoyable. Neither of us had ever been in Vegas so we were somewhat awed by the lights on the strip. Afterwards we went back to the restaurant. We had a steak and a beer and then headed for home. I left with $300 more than when we came. Jens broke even. Jens said, "hey that was fun let's do that again sometime".

I was still living in my apartment and walking the 10 blocks to and from work every day. I think this is the reason why felt good and that my health also stays good.

One day Ellen, the lady that works up front in the bakery, hollered at me and said" Hank you have a phone call". I said, "thanks Ellen, I'll take it back here" I picked up the phone and was pleasantly surprised when someone said" Hank, this is Joan. I said, "Well this is a surprise." I asked, "how are you"? She replied. "I'm fine but how are you"?" "I'm doing okay". Joan said, "to tell you the truth, I just had to hear your voice". We talked a little more and she said, "please keep in touch with me". I told her that I would and she said, "you know that I love you" "yes", I replied and also said, "Joan it is so nice to hear from you and I will keep in touch with you". I went back to work cleaning up for the end of the day. Later that day, Pete the boss said to Jens and me, "let's stop over at the bar and have a couple of beers We walked into the bar, there were several patrons and immediately they hollered at us, "come over and sit with us", to which we replied, "we'll be right over". We said, "you guys are buying aren't you? "Hell no", one of them replied. We really had a good time kidding each other, solving world problems, talking about sports and in general just having a good time.

We left the bar, each of us going in a different direction. I stopped at a newsstand and picked up a paper. On the way home I stopped at the diner to get something to eat. After getting home, I sat down at the kitchen table and began reading the newspaper that I had just bought. I started reading the front section and when I got to the middle section I suddenly saw this article. There was a picture of me. Underneath the picture it said, HAVE YOU SEEN THIS PERSON? IF YOU HAVE, PLEASE CALL—HE HAS BEEN MISSING FOR SEVERAL MONTHS. I was shocked. I just love it here, my boss Pete, Jens and so many of the people had become very good friends.

I knew then that I had to leave immediately. I am sure that a lot of people have already recognized me from the picture. I got out my bag and packed as much as I could, being sure to take a long the essentials. I wasn't even sure where I was going. I went to the bus station and just randomly picked the city of Pomona, California. The bus was scheduled to leave in about three hours. I found a bench that was somewhat remote from the main area of the bus station, trying to be as inconspicuous as possible. Someone had left a magazine on the bench, so I picked it up and read it, also kind of holding it up in front of my face so that no one would recognize me. It hurt to know that I had just walked out and left Pete at the bakery. He had been so good to me and I liked him as a friend, I'm sure he probably saw my picture in the paper and realized why I had left without saying a word to him. This would be another hurt that I would have to carry with me.

Finally, after what seemed to be an eternity, they announced that we were to board the bus. I took a seat as far back in the bus as I could, hoping not to be recognized. It was quite a long haul to Pomona, so I scooted down in the seat and put the Western hat over my face and I did actually go to sleep. After a couple of hours I woke up and just sat there looking out at the scenery. The ride seemed kind of rough in the back seat. We made a few stops picking up new passengers and dropping off those that had reached their destination.

At the next bus stop we switched buses and again headed for Pomona. I sat in the back of the bus and went to sleep again. I saw a couple of people staring at me as though they might have recognized me. We finally got to Pomona. I got off the bus and almost felt lost, not having any idea where to go, but I guess that would solve itself as it usually does.

In search of a place to stay for the night, I walked several blocks up the street. I walked past a building where there were four or five young guys sitting on the steps. As I walked by them they began taunting me, hollering at me, saying, "hey old man, where are you going"? I just ignored them and kept walking. They walked up behind me and said, "we are talking to you, you old bastard". I said to "them; leave me alone, I am not bothering you guys. "One of them said to me, "well you're bothering us". I kept walking and one of them gave me a shove. It angered me, I was just minding my own business, but they wouldn't leave me alone. They came at me and threatened to shove me again. My temper got the best of me and I hit one of them. That probably was a mistake because then they all started to beat me. They knocked me down, punched me in the face and kicked me in the ribs, but I managed to get up. I hit another one of them and gave him a bloody nose. They all came after me and I am not sure what happened because I lost consciousness. Someone saw what was happening and called 911. One of the guys that was after me said, "Somebody called the law, let's get the hell out of here". The police came, and called an ambulance and they took me to the emergency room at a nearby hospital. I was unconscious and not aware of anything. The gang stole my wallet which contained all of my identification, including my Medicare, supplementary insurance cards and all the cash I had on me. I did not have a Social Security card since I had memorized the numbers. Also I did not have a debit card since I didn't do any banking.

That left the police with no way of identifying me. They took my fingerprints and sent them to Washington to try to get identification. Later that day, they got their answer. "He is a Navy veteran and his name is Hank Anders". His last address is in Fort Dodge, Iowa. "We will contact the Sheriff's Department in Fort Dodge to see if they have any information about him". The Sheriff's Department in Fort Dodge replied to the inquiry telling them, "yes, he disappeared about a year ago". "His family has been trying to locate him and they will be happy to know that he is still alive". The Fort Dodge police also said, "we will immediately contact his family and have them get in touch with you".

After being contacted by the police, my family immediately got in touch with the police department in Pomona. They informed my son that I was in the hospital here in Pomona and was still in a coma. Of course, they also filled my family in on what had happened. My son said, "we will fly out there and get there as quickly as we can". 'The police also told them that doctors had said it was just a matter of time before I regained consciousness and that I should fully re-cover. There were cuts and bruises on my head plus a couple of broken ribs and I also had sustained a concussion.

After arriving there at the hospital and finding what my room number is my two sons walked into my hospital room. The doctor was in the room with me and he said to my sons, "I think he is beginning to regain consciousness". "He is moving around and is sort of mumbling". It would be a good idea if you would try to talk to him". "That sometimes helps them to come around".

I slowly regained consciousness and my eyes began to focus normally. I was surprised to see my two sons sitting there by my hospital bed. Actually, it was a tearful reunion and I was so very happy to see them. My oldest son said. "We will not question you now about what happened in the last year". "You are lucky to be alive".

"They must have stolen your wallet and all of your identification". My son said, "I know that you have Medicare and a supplementary policy". "I will call to the hospital and see if they can be in touch with Medicare and explain the situation to them in order to see what can be done about taking care of the hospital bill". I gave my son the name of the supplementary health insurance company. The hospital will be in touch with them and file a claim.

The doctor came back into the room and my son asked him, "When do you feel that he will be able to travel"? He replied, "we can probably release him in a couple of days but he had better see his family Dr., when he gets home". I said to the doctor, "that will be no problem and I will take care of that as soon as I get home". It was getting late in the day, so the boys told me, "you rest and we will be back in the morning". I'm sure they will contact everybody at home to let them know that I am all right'.

The boys visited me the next morning and told me that the hospital had talked with Medicare and that they could submit their bills. They also had contacted my supplementary insurance company and they also will take care of their portion of the hospital bill. My son told me, "when we get back home you will have to contact your insurance companies to get duplicate cards.

There is something we need to get decided. "Now, do you really want to go home with us"? I thought for a minute and said, "yes, I have put the family through enough". "Good, "they said, "They will all be very happy to hear this". They told me they would come back tomorrow and hopefully I would be released so we could head for home. As soon as they left, I went back to sleep and slept for hours. When I woke up, I felt much better and the headache was not as severe.

The next morning my sons came to pick me up. I was ready to go and had been for a couple of hours. I said, "let's stop someplace and have some breakfast". They found a restaurant and we had eggs, bacon, toast, hash browns and of course coffee. I was more hungry than I thought I was and breakfast sure hit the spot. The boys had rented a car and we proceeded to go to the airport. We checked in and, of course, went through the usual routine of being checked in. We boarded the plane and took off, heading for home. They asked me again, "you feel like talking or would you rather wait until we get home"? I said to them, "well, it's a long story". It would be better if we could sit down with the family and get it over with all at once". The boys agreed and then they looked at each other and said to me, "we might as well get it over with", "there is something that we need to tell you" "mom is not living alone, she has a guy living with her". I sat there in silence for a while. It was kind of a blow to me, but I said to my sons, "maybe this is why she always treated me so badly"

My son said, "we very seldom see her, but I think there are some things that need to be said between you". I was feeling kind of hurt, but then again, this reinforced my suspicions. My son said, "At any rate Dad the rest of the family will be very glad to see you". They both said to me" this has been a very hard year on all of us, but we can talk about that later".

One of the boys asked me again, "You do want to come home don't you"? I said, "Like I said before it is about time". I told them, "I am so sorry that I hurt the rest of you but I just didn't know what to do". "The abuse was so bad and continuous". "I could not live with it anymore". "Right now, I am just glad to be alive". 'Those guys almost killed me". "My ribs are so sore and at times I still have quite a headache but the doctor said that that will disappear in time". The boys did warn me, that the rest of the family will ask the question, "why".

The boys filled me in on everything at home the business seems to be going along smoothly, well run by both of them. So that was no worry. The grandchildren are all doing fine, but they are at the age that they don't get into much trouble.

We landed at the airport. he plane taxied up to the ramp and the passengers hurried off. We walked down the ramp, kind of tired, looking forward to getting home. I had arranged to stay at the home of one of my sons. When we got to the bottom of the ramp, I got a wonderful surprise. There, stood the whole family waiting for me. The tears welled up in my eyes and were running down my cheeks. This was more than I expected. It was a very happy reunion and I saw that most of my families were also very teary-eyed. After all the hugs and kisses, we left for my sons' home where they had planned to get together.

They had dinner ready, consisting of my favorites. After dinner, we all gathered in the living room. My daughters came over to me, gave me a hug and kiss on the cheek. My son, acting as the spokesman for the family said to me, "We are all so happy to have you home again, but we have a question for you and that question is, "why? "We are all aware of your reason for leaving but why didn't you talk to us"? "You have to know, that you put us all through hell". I responded to that by saying, "I am so sorry for hurting all of you, but I thought this was the better of two choices". "My other choice was suicide, and I thought that what I did was the least drastic". My family sat there in silence for a few moments. One of my daughters got up and said, "We will not question you any further about your reason for leaving because we understand". "We will continue seeing our mother even though we are not too happy about her current situation". "I know", I said. "That is all right". "You still love your mother and I ask that you please do stand by her".

One of my daughters said, "I hope when the dust gets settled here, that you will tell us about your experiences while you were gone". I agreed to do that and also told them how happy I am to be together with my family. My son said to me, "mom said she would like to talk to you; there are some things that need to be said. My reply to them was, "of course, I will do that".

I got up early the next morning and after having breakfast, I went to my wife's house. I rang the doorbell; she came to the door and asked me to come in. She said to me, "I suppose you hate me". I replied saying, "that's not important now". "There are some things we need to get settled". "I am sure you want the divorce", I said to her, "you get the divorce and I will not contest anything." "All I want is my car; a few of my tools and of course my clothes". "You can have the house and whatever else you want". She agreed that I should keep the car, my tools and clothes. She also said, "I have not touched anything in the bank since you've been gone." She said, "that is all yours including your retirement check". She gave me the keys to the car; I went to the garage, gathered up the tools that I wanted and also my clothes. I put them all in the car. I went back to the house and told her that I got what I wanted. That she could come and look to be sure that I didn't take anything else. She said, "no, that will not be necessary". I told her, "Anything that happened between us is now water under the bridge". "Let's forget it and get on with our lives". "The best of luck to you", I said, as I walked away.

I went to my son's house and told him what had transpired and he said, "I was afraid it was going to be a big blow up", "it was on my mind to have it out with her but I thought to myself what would that really accomplish. "I would rather leave all of that behind me and go forward with my life". I asked my son if it was possible to get the whole family together. I had something to say to them. Part of it was a rundown on my activities last year.

My family all gathered at my son's house. I thanked them all for coming and proceeded to tell them about the happenings while I was gone. I told them about hitching rides with semi drivers, the various jobs that I held and also my reason for traveling around to different locations. I also told them about the many friends that I met and worked for. As you know, "when the thugs beat me up in Pomona, I just felt that I could not go on any longer and it was time to come home". When I got home, there were some surprises that I had not ascertained".

"Now, there is something that I need to tell you". "The second job that I worked at was in Tucson, Arizona'. "I worked on a horse farm, owned by a lady." 'There was a bunkhouse there that I stayed in". "I ate my meals, breakfast, dinner and supper in the main house". "The main house is a large two-story home that had just recently been built". The owner of the horse farm was a lady named Joan Roth". About 60 years old and is a very nice person and, I might add. Quite attractive'." She was very nice to work for, and we became friends, nothing romantic, and she was just a happy-go-lucky type of person"." One night she asked me to go to a bar with her". "We went to the bar, met some of her friends and even danced a couple of times". "The next morning I got up, knowing that I had to leave because we were beginning to get too close". "My being married would not allow me to have a relationship with anyone else".

"I did leave the next morning but before I left she asked where I was going. I gave her the name of the city that I was going to, but that was the only information I gave because I myself, had no idea about what I was going to do". "I did find a job in the next city, which was Flagstaff". "Somehow she located me and came there to see me". "I knew that she did care for me and after that she managed to keep in touch with me". She is a wonderful person, and at that stage I began to care for her". "I would now like to get in touch with her". "When I got mugged in Pomona, they took everything I had, including her telephone number".

I asked my son, "do you have free long distance"? He said, "sure go ahead and use my phone". The rest of the family started to leave thinking that I wanted privacy. I told them, "I would like all of you to hear this". I found Joan's telephone number through information. I called the number and after two or three rings, Joan answered. I said, "Joan, this is Hank, "Right away, she said, "oh Hank, where are you"? "I have been so worried about you and was afraid I would never see you again". "Joan, I am here in Fort Dodge, Iowa with my family". "It's a long story about how I got here, but I will fill you in on that when I see you". "I can't wait to see you and tell you about everything that has happened". Joan said. "can I please come there right away to be with you"? I said, "I was hoping that you would ask". "I want you to meet my family"." Please drive carefully and also I can now say to you, I love you and can't wait to see you" "If you have a pen and paper, I will give you the address".

After talking to Joan, with my family listening in on the conversation, my family said, "she does sound like a very nice person and we will be anxiously looking forward to meeting her". I told my family, "you will even be more impressed when you meet her in person". I also said to them, "I have not mentioned anything to her before about love, although I knew she cared for me very much.

I knew that it would be a couple of days before Joan would get here, so I spent my entire time visiting with all of my family and getting my affairs in order. I had to get duplicate cards of my Social Security card, driver's license, Medicare and supplementary insurance cards. I also got a debit card from the bank and made arrangements for a different bank account.

The second day, after talking with Joan on the phone, I was at my son's house and the doorbell rang. I went to the door, opened it, and there stood Joan. We immediately embraced and kissed each other. I said to her, "you sure made good time". She looked at me with that impish little smile and said, "I drove straight through; I was in such a hurry to get here to be with you". I could see a tear streaming down her cheek and she said to me, "and I am so happy".

I introduced Joan to my son and his wife. They all hugged each other and said they are so happy to meet each other. I told them, "While Joan and I were together there on her horse ranch, I began to think quite a lot of her, but circumstances dictated that I remain sort of distant." Joan said to me, "I have loved you from the very first minute that I saw you". She said, "Hank, I will need to find a motel or hotel". My son overheard her and he said to Joan, "oh no you don't, you're staying right here with us". "We have a spare bedroom and we certainly welcome you". "Also that will give us a chance to know each other". Joan said, "thank you, I sure hope this won't inconvenience you". My son's wife said to Joan, "this will be no inconvenience, and you will be here so that the rest of the family can meet you and I know they will be as impressed with you as we are" Joan looked at me and I know from the look on her face, she was touched.

"Now that that's settled, I will help you carry your bags in" On the way to the car, Joan said to me, "your family is everything you said they were". "I hope they will accept me". I smiled at her and said, "They already have Joan".

That evening, all of my family gathered at my son's house. I introduced them to Joan and I could tell immediately that they were impressed with her. She has a wonderful personality and kindness just beams from her. I let Joan mingle with the family and it was obvious that they immediately liked her. My other son said, "dad, where did you meet Joan"? "She is exactly like you said she would be, only more". You can see from the expressions of all the family that they really liked Joan. Both of my daughter in-laws and my two daughters whispered to me, "You are lucky to have found her". I thanked them and went to Joan's side. She said to me, "they make me feel so at ease and I sure hope that I have made a good impression on them". I said to her, "I did not have the slightest doubt that they would love you".

"While you are all here, Joan and I would like to tell you that we plan to go back to Tucson to her horse ranch". As we have told you, Joan owns a horse ranch near Tucson"." I worked for her on the ranch and really enjoyed it". We went on to tell them, "This does not mean that we will be gone and out of touch with you". Joan and I will be contacting you quite regularly over the phone and we will come back to visit often". "Also, all of you are welcome to come and stay with us"." Joan's house is quite large and we have room for all of you and you can stay as long as you want". "We will be staying here for about a week before leaving for Arizona". My family stood in silence for a little bit and then they laughed, saying" we are very happy for both of you and you are very lucky Dad to have met Joan" needless to say, Joan and I stood there, hand in hand, quite teary-eyed and Joan said to them" thank you for your kind words I "I will be proud to be a part of this family and when we decide to get married, you are all invited and you can stay with us as long as you like"." I will be good to your dad." I have been in love with him from the minute that I saw him "I took my two sons aside and talked to them about the business. My words to them were, "you guys have done such a good job keeping the business going and in fact you have made it grow". The profits are very good and before I go, I'm going to entirely turn the business over to both of you". "It will be up to the two of you to run the business as partners". I am sure that you will get a long since you both have good heads on your shoulders and I'm also sure that you will not let pettiness interfere". 'They both smiled at me, and said, "you can count on us". "That's great", I said. "I will leave it up to the two of you to go to an attorney to have the legal papers drawn up".

Before we knew it, the week was over. There were some teary goodbyes, hugs and kisses and also many, "I love you"s said". We got in the car and headed back for Joan's ranch. Joan said to me, "well, we're off to a new adventure together". "I want you to know that I love you very deeply". "Joan, I also love you very much". As we were driving. Joan told me about her family and that they were all gone. She had been married once, when she was quite young but they mutually decided to go their own ways. Joan said, "I never had any children so what you see is what you get".

"It is just me, I have no family". I said to her, "but you are not alone anymore, you have me and I will always be at your side, loving and caring for you "Joan said, "you don't know how happy that makes me feel to hear you say that".

Shortly after arriving home, my son called and said to me, "the divorce proceedings have been finalized and are just waiting for your signature". "After signing the papers, the divorce will be completely final". He told me that he would send the papers to me via federal express and that I should receive them shortly. After a couple of days a federal express truck pulled into our driveway and delivered a large envelope containing the divorce papers. Joan and I sat down at the kitchen table, we read over the papers, I signed them and we drove into town, found a federal express office and sent them back.

We were sitting in the kitchen, Joan said to me, "There is something I want to talk to you about and I said, "Go ahead". She said, "You have never talked to me about or ever questioned me about my financial situation'. "I actually am quite a wealthy person". "I own oil stock, lots of it'. "I also own shares in two producing oil wells". "I am all by myself with no heirs and I want you to be my financial partner". "I will give half of my holdings over to you". "That is, of course, if you will approve". I said, "yes. but you should talk to your lawyer". Joan made an appointment with her attorney for later that afternoon. She explained the situation to him and said to him that Hank has never asked about my financial situation. The attorney said,

"I will make out he papers but you should not sign them for at least a week". Joan agreed. A week later she signed the papers, making it official. Then she looked at me with that little grin and asked me, "how does it feel to be a multimillionaire?'

Joan said, "Let's celebrate your freedom". We went to our favorite bar and had a couple of beers. Joan said, "do you know what this means"? "You are a free man and you are all mine". We had some work at home that needed to be done so when we got there Joan and I cleaned out the horse stalls and fed the horses. Joan said, "it's only 3 o'clock let's go riding for a while". We saddled up the horses and went riding on the trails through a wooded area and around the lake. We stopped in a small park to give the horses a rest and let them graze. We just sat there and talked. It was a pretty place and we just loved it there. Joan said, "this is what God gave us and I just love this place". "I certainly do to", I replied. The next morning Joan and I woke up early and just lay there in bed talking. Joan said, "I have an idea". "Okay, let's have it", I replied. Joan replied, "why don't we drive up to Iowa and visit your kids"? "Hey that's a great idea"." When shall we leave"? Joan said, "how about if we leave tomorrow until tomorrow, let's head out this afternoon". My reply was, "hey, I'm ready when you are".

We were on the road heading to Iowa, doing our usual joking and laughing. Joan asked me, "You know my real reason for wanting to go to Iowa"? I replied, "Well it came up so suddenly, Pm not really sure"." I hope you will like my idea", Joan said." We have all this money that we will never spend and I got the idea, why don't we use some of it to help your family". I looked at Joan and said, "Joan you are full of surprises and I love you". She said to me, "we will figure out how much to give them when we get there, but let's enjoy the rest of the trip together". As we drove down the road, we sang a couple of songs together and talked about when we were kids growing up and about my brothers and sisters, but Joan did not have any brothers or sisters, so she was especially interested in hearing about my growing up years. I told her about my Navy experiences and she told me about her college days. It was getting to be about 8 o'clock in the evening, so we stopped overnight, staying in a motel. It was up early the next morning and heading for Iowa again.

We got to my sons home in Iowa at about 8 o'clock in the morning. They were so surprised because we had not let them know we were coming. My son immediately got on the phone and called the rest of the family and in the a very short time they were all there, surprised, but happy.

We all visited together and just had fun being together. You could tell how much they love Joan by the way they all crowded around her and just enjoyed talking with her. After visiting for a while the family decided that they needed to go to their jobs and homes. Joan and I asked the two boys to stay for a while. After everybody had left we sat down around the kitchen table. One of my sons said, "what's up"? I told him that Joan and I had been talking and we thought that if it was okay we would like to pay off their companies' debts. Both of the boys looked at us in disbelief. Joan said, "let us know how much they are and we would give you the money to make your business free and clear". The boys said, "That's going to be in the neighborhood of $200,000". We told them, "that's alright, that's what we want to do". It was hard for them to believe that the burden of debt had been lifted from them. Joan and I both said to them, "you don't know how happy this makes us both feel to do that for you".

The next day Joan and I went to the construction business that my two daughter's husbands own. We went there early in the morning hoping to catch them both there in their office. They were surprised to see us and we can see from the expressions on their faces that they wondered why we were there, I said to them, "we are going to ask you a couple of questions that you may consider none of our business, but we have a reason and hope that you will bear with us"." First of all, how much debt does your business have"? They both looked at each other as though they were questioning whether or not to answer that question. Then they decided to tell us, that they had about $100,000 of debt. The next question I asked was, "is there equipment that you need that would help you in your business"? This one they readily answered. They said, "we could use about $75,000 worth of equipment". Joan said to them, "we will give you $200,000 to pay your debts and buy new equipment'. "This is a gift to you from us and we would be happy if you would accept". They said to us. "this is hard to believe but we certainly do accept and thank you from the bottom of our hearts".

That evening we met at my sons' house again, all of the families were there and the atmosphere was one of being overjoyed they thanked us over and over again and it made Joan and I so happy. Joan and I asked that we all meet in the restaurant of their choice the next morning to have breakfast together. We told them that after breakfast we would have to leave for home. So as we planned, we had breakfast together. Again it was a happy atmosphere. Joan and I stood up and said to them, "we have an announcement to make." "We will be getting married". We got a big cheer from all of them. Joan cold them, we haven't set a date or made any arrangements, but you will be getting invitations and you can all come and stay with us". We have plenty of room and we will pay all of your expenses including the trip to our home and back to your home".

We finished our breakfast and after all of the goodbyes, hugs and kisses, Joan and I left and started our trip home. We had gone a few miles and Joan said, "why don't we go to Branson and take in a couple of shows"? "We both like music, and I have wanted to go there for quite some time". "Hey. that's a good idea", I said. We got to Branson in late afternoon and had some difficulty finding a place to stay. Everything was pretty well booked up, but we finally found a room in a small motel and we were very happy to get it. We showered and changed clothes and set out to find a restaurant. After eating, we went to one of the shows and enjoyed it immensely. We went to another show which was equally entertaining. We went back to the motel and went to bed. We got up early the next morning, had breakfast and continued our trip home.

On the way home, we talked about the wedding plans. We both decided that we wanted a church wedding. Neither Joan nor I had any church affiliation. We just had not been going to church, so we thought that we should make church one of our priorities. Joan was more familiar with the area than I, so she named a couple of churches that she previously had attended. We decided that in the next couple of days we would pick one out and then attend the next Sunday. She said, "I don't want a big wedding with a wedding gown and all the frills." "We will invite a few of our friends and all of your family". Joan said, "we will get to all of that later". She and I decided that we would just take a leisurely drive home and not be in any hurry. Late in the afternoon, we stopped at a motel and got a room for the night. There was a restaurant nearby so Joan and I went there and had a snack before going back to the motel. When we got back to the motel, we had been there for just a few minutes when there was a knock at the door. Joan went to the door and started to open it but suddenly somebody just pushed their way in brandishing a gun. I quickly reached in my pocket and took out my pepper spray and sprayed him in the eyes. It shocked him, something he was not expecting. He certainly was not ready for that and when he reached to rub his eyes I went over quickly and buried my fist in his stomach as hard as I could. He doubled over and I twisted the gun out of his hand and almost at the same time Joan grabbed one of the heavier lamps and hit him over the head with the base of it. I pointed the gun at him and told him to lie on the floor and I said to him, "don't move a muscle". At the same time Joan called 911. It was his intent to rob us, but he said, "I had no intention of hurting anyone". I told the police officer that a few months ago, I had been mugged and since then I have carried a pepper spray in my pocket. He said that was a good idea and it sure saved us from possibly getting hurt. The police officer asked, "Do you intend to press charges"? Joan and I both responded almost simultaneously, "you darn right, we'll press charges".

After everything settled down, Joan and I went to bed. We must've laid there for a couple of hours talking about what had just transpired. We both marveled at how quickly we reacted and we also thank God for saving us.

The next morning we went to the police station and filed charges. We gave the police our names and address and telephone number and also told them if they needed anything from us we certainly would be available.

After leaving the police station we had breakfast and headed for home. We got home in the middle of the afternoon and we were very glad to be there. Joan and I walked out to the horse barn and got our usual greeting from the horses and you know we were just as happy to see them. I think this fits in with the saying, "there is no place like home". We walked hand in hand back to the house. As we walked. I said to Joan, "I love you Joan". She replied, "I love you too Hank".

We went to the living room and I noticed that Joan had a piano. I don't know why, but I hadn't noticed it before. I asked her, "Do you play the piano"? To which she replied, "Sure, sit down and I'll play something for you. As we had mentioned before, we both like music very much, so as Joan was playing, we began singing together. Joan said, "that was fun, but I think I will teach you to harmonize with me, that would be even more fun". We worked on the singing together, but the harmonizing did not come easy for me, but we kept practicing and finally we were singing quite well together.

As we had talked earlier, we attended a church that Joan had picked out. During the services they sang several songs. Joan and I sat in a pew singing and of course, we harmonized as we had practiced at home. Some of the people sitting near said, "you two sing very well together". "Maybe we can get you to sing for us some Sunday". We had not counted on doing that, but we talked about it and thought it might be fun. We began to practice in earnest and it seemed that we got a little better all the time.

We went to church one Sunday morning and a lady walked up to us and asked, "would you and Joan sing the song, "IN THE GARDEN" for us today"? Somewhat hesitantly, we said, "sure, we will do our best". It went pretty well for us and we got several compliments from the congregation. After church, we decided that this is the church that we should be married in.

When we got home, we talked about setting a date to be married. We decided to be married in a month. So that meant sending out invitations and getting everything ready. We decided to have a reception in the community building not too far from the church. We would hire a band to play at the reception and hope that everyone would dance with us. We were doing our best to make this a fun affair, full of happiness and laughter.

Joan and I met with the minister to discuss our wedding plans and set a date that would fit his schedule. He was a happy go lucky type of person and you could see that he smiled and laughed easily. He said, "I heard you sing in church and it was beautiful and hope you will continue coming and become members of our church". We told him, "This is what we plan to do". We set a wedding date, about a month later which was on a Friday night. We hired a band and made arrangements with a caterer. We also arranged to rent the community building for that evening,

We spent most of the day making out invitations and deciding who to send them to. Joan had them printed and we thought they were very nice. We got them all done and Joan said to me, "well it looks like we are all set except planning our honeymoon". "Where would you like to go Joan"? I said to her, "we can go to Hawaii; I was there while I was in the Navy". "It is a beautiful place". "I was also stationed in New York city". "I think you would really enjoy it'. "There are so many places to sec". Joan said, "New York City it is". I said to her, "if that makes you happy, I will be happy too".

We pretty much stayed at home that month before the wedding. It seemed that we were happy just to be together and our love for each other just seemed to grow. Some of our friends would stop over and we had such a good time visiting, walking around the ranch, having a beer or two and just being friends.

As the wedding day drew near, my family began to arrive and we were all so happy to be together. There were a couple of days before the wedding, so Joanne I took them out to eat and we all went horseback riding down the trail around the lake and everybody seemed to enjoy it. My sons and I went fishing at the lake. Joan and the girls went shopping. While fishing, we caught several bass and we did a lot of talking, filling me in on how the business was going, which was quite well. I showed them around the ranch and they said to me, "we can see why you like it so well here". "It is a beautiful place". Soon the wedding day was here. I asked both my sons to serve as best men. Joan asked my two daughters to serve as maids of honor, which they did. Joan and I stood before the minister as he started with the words, "we are gathered here today, before

God, to join Joan and Hank in holy matrimony". He proceeded to finish the ceremony and the wedding was just beautiful.

After the ceremony, we went to the community building where the reception was being held. There were so many people there and the room was filled with laughter and much happiness. Most of the people stood up with accolades for Joan and I. Some of the things they said were quite touching. I got up and addressed the crowd and said to them, "Joan and I are so happy that you came to our wedding." "We are so blessed with having so many good friends and relatives here". Joan also stood up, "I am so happy for all of you and having you as such good friends, but I'll tell you I am so thankful and happy to have my new family here". "They are like sons and daughters to me"." I thank God for the many blessings he has given us and we love all of you". When Joan was finished, the tears were streaming down her face and I could feel my heart just bursting with love for her. Later in the evening, Joan and I went out to the car, ready to leave on our honeymoon. Most of the people came out and surrounded us. They wished us every bit of happiness and a safe journey. Joan and I got in the car and drove away into our honeymoon and our new life together. Our love for each other continues to blossom even further. We continue to live on the horse ranch, enjoying our family and friends. Joan calls them her family. We will always thank God for the life he has given us and we both hope that God will bless everyone.

www.ingramcontent.com/pod-product-compliance
Lightning Source LLC
LaVergne TN
LVHW041541060526
838200LV00037B/1081